# T.H.I.N.K. More

# T.H.I.N.K. More™

## The Key to
## Business Communication
## SUCCESS

by

Jan Dyer O'Neil

# T.H.I.N.K. More™
## The Key to Business Communication SUCCESS

© 2018 Jan D. O'Neil

Published in New York, New York, by Morgan James Publishing. Morgan James is a trademark of Morgan James, LLC. www.MorganJamesPublishing.com

The Morgan James Speakers Group can bring authors to your live event. For more information or to book an event visit The Morgan James Speakers Group at www.TheMorganJamesSpeakersGroup.com.

ISBN 9781630475857 paperback
ISBN 9781630475864 eBook
Library of Congress Control Number: 2015902713

**Illustrations:** Pages 20, 49, 77, 87, 92, 138, and 144 illustrations by Frank Ramspott (iStock by Getty Images). Page 23 illustration by Patrick W. Dennis. Pages 30, 32, 85, and 110 illustrations by Adam Dunn. Page 62 illustration by LEOcrafts (iStock). Page 134 illustration by Owattaphotos (iStock). Pages 45, 73, 89, 105, and 114 illustrated by the author.

**Editors:** Diane Giombetti Clue and Michelle Gaudet

**Photograph of Jan Dyer O'Neil:** Glenn Geise

**Book Cover Design:** Patrick W. Dennis

**Interior Design:** Patrick W. Dennis

In an effort to support local communities, raise awareness and funds, Morgan James Publishing donates a percentage of all book sales for the life of each book to Habitat for Humanity Peninsula and Greater Williamsburg.

Get involved today! Visit
www.MorganJamesBuilds.com

# CONTENTS

# Quotes for Thinking

"I very rarely think in words at all. A thought comes, and I may try to express it in words afterwards."

—Albert Einstein

"I'm a great believer that any tool that enhances communication has profound effects in terms of how people can learn from each other, and how they can achieve the kind of freedoms that they're interested in."

—Bill Gates

"Technology is nothing. What's important is that you have a faith in people, that they're basically good and smart, and if you give them tools, they'll do wonderful things with them."

—Steve Jobs

"Machines might give us more time to think but will never do our thinking for us."

—Thomas J. Watson Jr.

# Introduction
# Why T.H.I.N.K.?

You're lucky. You're not living one hundred years ago when your only choices of communication were a meeting, letter, or telephone call. We are very fortunate to have many means of sharing information. Imagine, you can post your thoughts to the world, Facetime with someone halfway around the world, and send an e-mail to millions throughout the world. Electronics have empowered us with astounding communication tools, which have immensely improved how we interact and thrive. Can we use these tools better? The answer is yes. We know more today in neuroscience and psychology about *how we work* to improve *how we work*. How can communication nirvana be achieved? The answer is not found looking forward to the future—the answer lies in taking a step backward before BC.

**We haven't changed much.** What's the difference between you and our primitive ancestors? You wear better clothing and shoes and, of course, you bathe with soap! According to anthropologists, the human brain has not changed in more than 100,000 years. How your brain operates today is comparable to the way our courageous ancestors' did. What is the most interesting aspect about our likeness to them? It's the reality that the human brain and body are built foremost for survival, not happiness.

**Surviving and thriving today.** As Maslow's hierarchy of needs states, when our physical (air, water, and food) and safety needs are met, we are then allowed to experience our wants for love and belonging, self-esteem, and self-actualization. Unlike our ancestors, for most of us, our physical and safety needs are often met, resulting in our continuous focus on love, self-esteem, and self-actualization. Though, regardless of whether our needs are met, underneath our loincloth or suit, we are foremost a primitive being who is *always* in survival mode. In other words, our ancestors' instinctive traits will *always* take precedence in our daily actions.

**Our great similarities.** We've all heard about our "fight or flight" similarity with our hardy ancestors; of course, we share much more. Additional key attributes we have in common with them are a sophisticated alert system for protection, a body designed for physical activity, eyes for seeking food or predators, and an extremely powerful gratification system. Though you no longer use your alert system to protect yourself from predators, your physical skills to run from them, your eyes to seek out wild beasts, or a gratification system to search for food—you still operate the same way. As were our brave ancestors, we are on continuous alert, highly visual and physical, and seek gratification all day long.

Accepting and working with our ancestors' attributes, whether these traits are a limitation or advantage, empowers us to live and work better.

**You're on continuous alert.** As with our ancestors, our brain is unable to manage more than one communication task at a time, and it's unable to shut off its sophisticated alert system unless we're asleep. What impact do these two traits have on us today? The Internet and electronics challenge us not only by presenting the opportunity to multitask communication, but also by alerting us when someone wants our attention. Unfortunately, the reality is we can't multitask communication—and when we try, according to research, we increase our error rate by 50 percent. Though our extraordinary alert system served us well when we needed to be aware of dangerous beasts, alerts from electronics are toying with this system. Intrusive alerts are challenging our ability to stay focused, which is affecting our decision-making, productivity, and well-being. Even if we've met all the needs on Maslow's hierarchy, we are still unable to control the fact that our brain is on constant alert status; in other words, we're wired to worry. Imagine this scenario: you're with your loved one enjoying one other's company immensely, yet when you hear a sound alert from an electronic, you can't help but wonder, who can it be?

**You love to be physical.** Look at those legs, arms, and torso: you're meant to stand, run, walk, and talk. In fact, when asked in a survey, participants said their top activities were making love, working out, and talking. Staring at a screen, reading message after message, switching screens, and multitasking creates unnecessary stress. Research has proven that exercise helps us feel better physically and mentally. Furthermore, conversation is our third favorite activity. What do people like to talk about most? Ourselves, of course!

**You're highly visual.** Like our keen ancestors, we bond through reading body language, which helps us guess at the hidden emotions that are vital in communicating. Research has confirmed this fact with hundreds of studies on body language. When you are speaking in front of others, you're providing the audience with your body's powerful and unconscious cues. Therefore, when we communicate via telephone or messaging, these key cues are not visible, which alters the exchange of information. And, even though a virtual meeting is better than a phone conversation, studies have proven that meetings are far more productive when everyone is in the conference room.

**You're always seeking gratification.** And finally, there is a significant similarity we share with our ancestors: we seek constant gratification through rewards, which give us energy and pleasure. We like to be rewarded, whether it's big or small. Rewards come in many different ways, from purchasing a new car to sending an e-mail. Yes, you read that correctly. Sending an e-mail or text gives us a feeling of accomplishment. Regardless if the manner in which you're communicating is often inefficient, your brain is sending positive signals that you've accomplished a task. You can easily understand why many of us enjoy working with e-mail and texting. Though, are we always gratified with technology? Let's answer this question in the next paragraph.

**Do you prefer primitive tools or technology?** Years ago, scientists predicted numerous changes in how we would live after the year 2000. These predictions included eating meals in pill form, working in a paperless office, and commuting less with the explosion of the virtual office. Why didn't all of those predictions about technology come to realization? According to renowned futurist and physicist, Dr. Michio Kaku, when we experience a conflict between modern technology and the desires of our primitive ancestors, these primitive desires win each time, which he refers to as the *Caveman Principle*. For instance, the proud caveperson may have boasted about the animal he killed, as you may boast about the turkey you cooked, yet talking and showing are very different. We prefer to see "proof of kill"; in other words, we want to see the tantalizing turkey. Obviously, our senses are more engaged in the physical world than in the virtual world. This fact easily explains why we continue to receive catalogs, go to museums, travel around the world, attend sporting events, and print documents.

**What is your ultimate goal in business?** Do you seek better relationships? Do you seek financial success? Do you seek a better business life? Whether your objective is to be promoted to manager or mastermind a billion dollar organization, communication is foremost. This book is dedicated to sharing information on improving your communication skills from process to punctuation. You'll learn how to benefit from understanding the strengths and weaknesses of your inner caveperson, as well as capitalize on the power that technology has to offer. Overall, you'll read ideas about mindful communication, which are fueled by neuroscience and psychology to help you work better, live better, and think more!

# Chapter 1

# Working Like It's 1999

**T**he power of *think*. When did the highly marketable word *think* become a motivator in business? Its origin dates back over one hundred years ago. In the early 1900s, a young sales manager named Thomas J. Watson Sr. was determined to inspire his sales force at the offices of National Cash Register, *NCR*. During a meeting, Watson found that his managers did not have any good ideas about how to improve the business. He became frustrated, strode to the front of the room and said, "The trouble with every one of us is that we don't think enough." He asked his team to think more and soon after, placards of this powerful word appeared on desks throughout the office. Later at IBM, he inspired teams at the company with the same concept. Thomas Watson Sr. believed, "Knowledge is the result of thought, and thought is the keynote of success in this business or any business." Over the years, the word *think* has been synonymous with IBM from products to slogans. Apple capitalized on IBM's *think* to ask us to "Think Different." Even Google is using *think*

1

as a source for insights, trends, and research. What's next? A better T.H.I.N.K.

**What is T.H.I.N.K.?** It's not only a powerful, thought-provoking word, but also a smart acronym to maximize your day-to-day communication objectives. T.H.I.N.K. represents five keywords that target essential elements of mindful communication. What is mindful communication? It's simply being aware of how you're communicating, whether you're listening, speaking, or writing. On that point, the five keywords of the T.H.I.N.K. acronym embody the aspects of productive, secure, focused, creative, and proper communication. Though the elements of T.H.I.N.K. are presented throughout this book, this chapter focuses on defining this empowering acronym by taking a trip back in time to business communication in 1999.

**Why 1999?** Well, it certainly wasn't for the grunge look or the Rachel haircut! In the '90s, communication technology began to enter into the American business office. Personal computers, cell phones, the Internet, and e-mail were well on their way to becoming essential tools for professionals. However, before these technologies became mainstream, your communication choices were the telephone, meeting, correspondence, or fax machine. Letters and memorandums were sent sparingly because administrative assistants or secretaries were responsible for recording, typing, and distributing correspondence. Therefore, the cost of sending it "in writing" was very expensive. What did professionals rely primarily on to communicate? As many of you know, the answer is "conversation."

**How did you manage communication without the Internet or a smartphone?** Again, before e-mail, you only sent information on paper when you absolutely, positively had to. You had no choice but to converse on a landline, which kept you at your desk. You shared information through meetings (telephone or in person) and essential documents. Often, an administrative assistant kept notes at the meeting and later typed and distributed these notes through interoffice envelopes. You received hard copies (paper) of everything, which included letters, reports, and junk mail. If you had to work late, you did so at the office. When you left the office, it was rare to receive telephone calls after business hours.

**Today, we are "heavily communicated."** We receive information around the clock on electronic devices from computers, tablets, smartphones, smartwatches, and more. You choose how you want to communicate, whether it's conversation, text, e-mail, post, or paper. You can make a business call at your desk, in your car, or on a mountain. You can share information online any time of day or night. Overall, the advantages of communicating today are excellent speed, ease of distribution, and infinite storage. Of course, we all understand the disadvantages of these devices, which include messaging overload, miscommunication, low productivity, and data breaches. Can we improve our business day by using a smart mix of communication tools from conversation to e-mail and posting to paper? The answer is yes!

**How can you achieve communication nirvana?** Just T.H.I.N.K. Again, this powerful acronym represents five keywords that target essential elements of mindful communication. Using T.H.I.N.K. as a communications management tool ensures the following results:

- **T**alk More, Type Less – Smarter productivity
- **H**andle Content with Care – Secured information
- **I**nvite Information In – Improved focus
- **N**ote – Greater creativity and memory
- **K**indness – Better business relationships

**What makes T.H.I.N.K. a smart business management tool?** T.H.I.N.K. is not only effortless to remember and apply, but it's also a smart management tool for you, your team, and your entire organization. T.H.I.N.K. is supported by ten smart and sensible guidelines, which are based on years of research in numerous fields.

**Let's go back in time.** Each acronym of T.H.I.N.K. is presented in a three-part format, which includes an entertaining business scenario in 1999 versus today, a comparison overview, and as stated, smart guidelines. Please note, the following stories are fictional and do not depict any actual person or company. However, you may find several instances in these brief scenarios that are similar to your own experiences at the office.

# T.H.I.N.K. – Talk
## Scenario 1: Communicating Your Great Idea

**1999:** You're driving to work and singing at the top of your lungs to Prince's finale to the 20th century, "1999," which is blaring through the speakers of your car. As you drive to the office, you think of an incredible idea: it brings a huge smile to your face. The idea is so awesome, you look in the rearview mirror and say, "Wow, I'm brilliant." You plan to share the idea with your boss the moment you step through the office doors. You're thinking to yourself; you'll probably get a bonus for this concept. Hey, you may even be promoted! Feeling so awesome, you pick up two coffee drinks, including a specialty one for your boss. At the office, you present your boss with not only her favorite hot beverage, but also with your idea that she agrees is fantastic. She provides you with additional insights, which add value to your concept. At the end of the conversation she says,

"Please put that in writing." Once the meeting is finished, you dictate the idea to your assistant, who types the memorandum and delivers it to your boss. Overall time communicating: 90 minutes within one day (uninterrupted).

**Today:** You're at the gym working out and rocking out to Prince's "1999" on your iPhone. As you walk on the treadmill, an incredible idea pops into your mind, which brings a huge smile to your face. You look in the mirror at the gym and say, "Wow, I'm brilliant." You plan to send your boss an e-mail about the idea the moment you step through the office doors. You're thinking to yourself; you'll probably get a bonus for this concept. Hey, you may even be promoted! Feeling so awesome, you treat yourself to your favorite coffee drink as you drive to the office. The moment you arrive at work, you begin typing the best e-mail you've ever sent to your boss. It takes you one hour to type and, after 20 minutes of editing, you press the Send button with confidence. Your boss is going to be amazed. Two days later, your boss finally responds. Twelve e-mails are sent back and forth until your boss recommends the two of you should meet to discuss the idea further. During the meeting, she provides you with additional insights, which add value to your concept. At the end of the conversation she says, "Please resend your e-mail to me with the edits we discussed." Overall time communicating: three hours and 35 minutes within three days.

### Communication Options in 1999 versus Today

**1999:** Your only communication options were conversing, mailing a paper letter or memo, or faxing a document. Mailing an interoffice memorandum or letter was costly; therefore, you'd opt to discuss the matter. After conversing, if the information was of great importance, you'd have your assistant type, print, and distribute the document. Outcome: you spent less time typing and more time talking, collaborating, thinking, and creating.

**Today:** With so many communication options, we often rely on the ease of e-mail, from quick "hellos" to paragraphs of content. You don't need a secretary because everyone can type and send his or her own messages (e-mail). Outcome: you spend more time typing and less time talking, collaborating, thinking, and creating.

# Talk More, Type Less: Smarter Productivity

**Talking is healthy, productive, and wise.** The following facts, ideas, and research prove that using your vocal cords more, rather than typing, enables you to work more efficiently and effectively, in other words, just smarter! Yes, you'll find a number of the following ideas are good common sense too.

## • Satisfying, Productive Communication

**Talking makes you happy.** A study on happiness lead by Harvard University psychologists Matthew A. Killingsworth and Daniel T. Gilbert had interesting findings. They developed an iPhone app used to "track your happiness." The study contacted 2,250 volunteers at random intervals to ask how happy they were during a particular activity, as well as what they were thinking. What were the results? People were happiest when making love, exercising, or engaging in conversation. A great reason to talk more!

**Looking to communicate faster?** The average business professional types at 38-40 words per minute or WPM; however, he or she speaks at 125-160 WPM. Obviously, you converse more than three times faster than you type; therefore, you're more efficient when you speak. Why spend 20 minutes typing a message when you can spend five minutes speaking it?

**Wait!** We talk at 160 WPM and type at 40 WPM, yet we read at 300 WPM. Isn't it just as fast to share information by typing (40 WPM) and reading (300 WPM), which results in an average transfer of information at 170 WPM? The answer depends on the information you're sharing. You'll read more about the importance of choosing the most effective way to communicate each time you share information.

**Working in real time.** Here's another good reason to talk more: you don't have to wait. With e-mail or text, you're often waiting for a response. In some instances, you're on alert waiting for a reply. It's a little like sitting in the doctor's office waiting for your name to be called. The "e-mail waiting room" can be stressful and time-consuming. The healthier side is of communicating is conversation, because the exchange is occurring right at the moment.

**Avoiding "e-mail tennis."** Another challenging aspect of messaging is when you're experiencing a game of "e-mail tennis." In the game of tennis, the score love-love is considered to be pointless, which is similar to the electronic text version. What exacerbates this messaging game? It's when you have more than two people playing: you've got nine! E-mail and texting are often inefficient in the exchange of information. These means of communication can waste time and energy throughout the business day. Although, when messaging is used effectively, it is a very powerful means of sharing information.

## • Improving Understanding and Collaboration
**Conversation is king!** Conversing more with others rather than sending e-mail, texting, or posting content; you're also

improving on collaboration. This lively exchange of information results in fewer misunderstandings and even more happiness.

**What!** Have you ever opened an e-mail, read it, and felt the blood in your body quickly travel up to your face, because you were shocked by what the reader had written? Then you realized that you misunderstood the tone the person was conveying in the communication (ouch). As you know, another wonderful aspect of conversation is the ability to hear the tone in the speaker's voice. Misunderstandings are resolved quickly, unless the person you're speaking with is talking in ALL CAPS. Insert your laugh here!

**Huh?** Tone isn't the only challenge with e-mail and text: there's also the risk of misinterpretation due to poor writing skills. Have you ever read an e-mail several times to find you were unable to understand the point the writer was conveying? Then, you spoke with the person, and within moments of conversing, you understood immediately. Again, with conversation, misunderstandings are clarified quickly. If your content is open to misinterpretation, enjoy the clarity that conversation brings.

**What is the most effective way to communicate?** When sharing information and building social connections, the tools of communication are ranked as follows: conversation via the phone is good, a virtual meeting is better, and a face-to-face meeting is the most effective. When we meet with others in person, eye contact and body language play a great role in understanding one another. According to UCLA psychology professor Albert Mehrabina, body language is key. His research found that 55 percent of what you convey when you speak comes from your body language, 38 percent is from your tone of voice, and only 7 percent is from the words you choose. We should never underestimate the power of our presence!

## • Empowering Messaging and Posting

**Messaging is like salt: it's best used sparingly.** Before e-mail, IM, and texting entered the office; organizations relied on interoffice memorandums and letters to communicate key information to employees, clients, customers, and vendors. As mentioned earlier, because the cost of typing, copying, and distributing was so expensive; memorandums and letters were mailed when absolutely necessary. Professionals relied primarily on conversations to share and create: directives, ideas, and solutions from these meetings were then placed in writing. Correspondence was sent mainly to share essential information.

**Master messaging (e-mail) and power posting.** Rather than using messaging to "converse" or share information, rely more on the power of posting. Share and create more with conversation and document directives, ideas, and outcomes. When distributing documentation electronically, it's best to use e-mail primarily for external communication and posting for internal communication.

**Posting.** Internal communication, whether colleagues are located in the same building or thousands of miles away, is best shared by posting (uploading) content on a secured, shared platform. Several advantages of posting are easy access, secure content, and less data storage required. Furthermore, posting is beneficial when communicating with external partners as well.

**Messaging.** E-mail is more powerful when it's used strictly for internal meeting invitations, internal posting announcements, and external communications that do not require a response.

**What's the outcome?** You'll stop the never-ending whirlwind of unnecessary internal e-mail. You'll collaborate wiser, communicate effectively, and experience less stress.

**More!** In Chapter 2, you'll learn more about managing e-mail and smart communications management.

# T.H.I.N.K. MORE

## Life without E-mail

**Less stress and more focus.** In a revealing study lead by the professor of informatics at UC Irvine, Gloria Mark, participants who did not use e-mail for five business days experienced less stress, focused longer on their tasks, and multitasked less. During the study, participants' heart rates and software usage were monitored with e-mail usage (for baseline data) and without e-mail. When not using e-mail, these suburban business professionals engaged in more face-to-face interactions and telephone conversations, which they viewed as a benefit. In addition, they were able to spend longer periods of time on a task and focus more intently on their work.

**What was the difference in heart rates?** The study found that participants who read e-mail all day changed screens twice as often and were in a steady "high alert" state with more constant heart rates. Participants who did not use e-mail experienced more natural, variable heart rates.

**Is it urgent?** Avoid sending "urgent" messages. How you manage important and urgent information is critical to your business relationships, as well as your career. Rather than delivering urgent subject matter in an e-mail, use the power of your voice or presence to ensure your message is conveyed and assimilated appropriately. For large organizations, rely on the chain of command to communicate proprietary, urgent matters and confirm with documentation that's posted.

**You might be thinking.** "Everyone in my office uses e-mail to converse and share information, even my boss."

Each of us has the opportunity to set a good example when we communicate. When a colleague, client, customer, or vendor sends a "conversational" e-mail; respond to him or her with a conversation in person or on the phone. If they complain, simply explain your goal of improving communication by sharing and creating more with conversation and documenting only directives, ideas, and outcomes. Overall, the less you send, the less you'll receive, and the more you'll achieve.

**Proof it works!** What happened when a London-based company's executive team wanted to increase their organization's efficiency? An analysis suggested that too much e-mail usage might be a part of the problem. What did they do? Rather than deploying e-mail management tools to improve, the team decided to manage communication as if it were an industrial process. They focused on reducing efficiency killers, which were e-mail messages that were confusing, unnecessary, and ineffective. After the executives had participated in training to limit messaging and use more effective means to communicate, they were able to reduce e-mail output by 54 percent within three months. In addition, their actions had an effect on the entire company: companywide e-mail output was reduced by 64 percent. They gained 10,400 in work hours (annual), which translated to a 7 percent increase in productivity.

# T.H.I.N.K. – Handle
## Scenario 2: A Multi-Million Dollar Concept

**Today:** David's office is totally awesome: colorful surfboards hang on the walls, an array of fish swim in a large aquarium, and a beautiful wooden desk faces a window with an ocean view. He's the director of marketing for an entertainment software company, Wayway Cool. David has an awesome idea for a rockstar hologram software program, which allows consumers to watch vintage concerts in 3D at home. He types a detailed proprietary and confidential e-mail about the program and sends it to his boss Clarissa, vice president of marketing. She is intrigued by the idea and forwards the e-mail to Chad, vice president of sales. Chad sends Clarissa an e-mail agreeing that it's a "way cool" idea. Chad then forwards Clarissa's original e-mail to Ellen, the company's biggest account. Ellen likes the idea too, yet wants to know if Wayway Cool's competitor can develop a comparable program for less cost and meet the same delivery date. Ellen creates a new e-mail, copies confidential content from Chad's message, and sends it to Wayway Cool's biggest competitor. What was the outcome? David, Chad, and Clarissa discover their company's biggest competitor created a very similar program, beat them to the marketplace, and launched a hologram concert featuring the album *Some Girls* by the Rolling Stones. The competitor's sales skyrocket, and they are launching a new program with the album, *Bruce Springsteen & the E-Street Band Live in NYC*. Ugh!

**1999:** David's office is totally awesome: colorful surfboards hang on the walls, an array of fish swim in a large aquarium, and a beautiful wooden desk faces a window with an ocean view. He's the director of marketing for an entertainment software company, Wayway Cool. David has an awesome idea for a rockstar hologram software program, which allows consumers to enjoy vintage concerts in 3D at home. After meeting about the idea with his boss, Clarissa, the vice president of marketing, he dictates a memorandum to his assistant. She types and prints the document, marks it "proprietary and confidential," and sends the memo via interoffice envelope to his boss. Clarissa is thrilled to receive Dave's idea in writing. She then hand-delivers a copy of the memo to Chad, vice president of sales. Chad screams, "Way cool" and convinces Clarissa that he must contact the company's number-one account to discuss retail opportunities for "Hologram Rock." What was the outcome? Just in time for the holidays, Wayway Cool releases a hologram concert featuring the album *Some Girls* by the Rolling Stones and sales at the company skyrocket! Wayway Cool receives requests from every country and rock 'n roll band in the world to make the program for their band's concerts. David, Clarissa, and Chad all received sizable bonuses and purchased beautiful luxury cars.

### Confidential Content in 1999 versus Today

**1999:** Documents marked confidential and proprietary were not widely distributed. Outcome: Confidential and proprietary information was easily kept private and secure. **Today:** The Send key makes it very easy to distribute confidential and proprietary information to fellow team members. Outcome: Confidential and proprietary information is EVERYWHERE on the Internet.

# Handle Content with Care: Secured Information

**BE (Before E-mail).** In the good old days, proprietary and confidential information was not easily obtainable. This type of content was either discussed privately or placed on paper with limited distribution. If it was on paper, it was serious business, and stamped "proprietary and confidential," which easily expressed to the reader, "do not duplicate or forward." Today, the Internet makes it extremely easy for information to be distributed.

Subsequently, the business world has experienced a change in the status of proprietary and confidential information when this content is sent via e-mail. Although e-mail is protected under the Fourth Amendment of the U.S. Constitution and is governed by the "reasonable expectation of privacy" standard, its ability to transfer may lessen the expectation of privacy compared to other forms of communication. The following provides ideas on managing personal, proprietary, and confidential content.

## • Protecting Proprietary/Confidential Content

**The old saying.** What's the best way to manage proprietary and confidential information? As the old saying goes, if you don't want something repeated, don't repeat it. With electronic text, the saying changes: if you don't want everyone to read it, don't send or post it! To ensure you're not sending or posting sensitive information over electronic devices, consult with colleagues in defining how content should be managed electronically. Overall, your company's policy on managing proprietary and confidential information should consider guidelines for the following:

- Composing and approval of drafts
- Distributing/forwarding documents
- Filing/posting documents
- Deleting documents and files

**What are proprietary and confidential data?** The basic definition of proprietary information is "belonging to a proprietor." Proprietary data is key information owned by a company that gives the organization a competitive advantage. If you're a knowledge employee, you're working with proprietary information all day. What is confidential data? Confidential information is company or other organizational data that is considered private. It's not intended to be disclosed outside the context of the company or organization.

**Conversation results in less information at risk.** As you learned at the opening of this chapter, you're more efficient in the exchange of information when you avoid using e-mail and texting to converse. Another key benefit or "icing on the cake" of conversing is the reduced risk of an information breach.

## • Safeguarding Personal, Private Information

**Privacy, please.** At the office, if you're sending personal e-mail or text messages with your company's URL or its electronics (traveling or home), these messages can become the property of the company. Many professionals have been dismissed from their positions for not only using company property for personal reasons, but also for the content of their messages. Using your own electronics for personal communication is wise.

**Special Note:** The integrity of a company is a key to its success. When unprofessional e-mail, text messages, and postings are leaked to the press; these communications can harm the company's image. Smart organizations ensure that external corporate messages are managed strategically and appropriately.

**One Last Note:** Executives may want to consider the effects of their own personal communication in regard to the company's image. Here's a good example of the reason why. A while back, an executive of a large grocery store chain was posting comments on a major finance company's Internet bulletin board. He was doing so under an alias, which was his wife's name spelled backwards. On the postings, this CEO not only championed his company's stock, but also occasionally blasted his competitor. What happened? He was caught! His alias surfaced in the footnote of a 40-page court document filed by lawyers for the Federal Trade Commission. A more humorous note about the ordeal is that he even posted a comment about his haircut, ". . . I think he looks cute!"

# T.H.I.N.K. – Invite

## Scenario 3: Meeting the Important Deadline

**1999:** It's 9 a.m. You're enjoying a cup of coffee and reading about the Y2K bug in the newspaper before you begin editing a report. The report is due on your boss's desk at the end of the business day. Not a problem: you have plenty of time to get it finished. You review the concept, flow, and timelines. As you edit, you're interrupted by three telephone calls, which you stop to answer each time. In addition, two colleagues stop at your desk to chat. Again, you're not concerned: the report will be completed by lunch. You ask a colleague to review it as well, and she makes a few edits. You update the report and head off for lunch with friends. When you return, you review it one more time and drop it on the boss's desk hours before the deadline. Yeah, you're that good.

**Today:** It's 9.a.m. You're drinking a cup of coffee as you read your e-mail. One keeps popping up after the next. You know you've got a report to finish, but you have 12 e-mails left before you can start to review it. You begin to work on the report and "beep," a text on your mobile phone has captured your attention. Five minutes later, "beep," another e-mail has caught your attention too; unfortunately, the message has nothing to do with you. It's noon, and you grab lunch at the fast-food restaurant down the street as you catch up on personal text messages and check out your Facebook page. Within 20 minutes, you return to work to get the report done. Fifty-seven more "beeps" later from e-mail and text alerts, you nearly have the report complete. You read it one more time, and at 5:30 p.m., you press the Send button and e-mail the report to your boss. Whew, that was close.

### Focusing on Tasks Today versus 1999

**Today:** Employees manage more than 120 e-mails per day, along with unplanned meetings, telephone calls, and text messages. Outcome: Your focus is challenged throughout the day from handling impromptu meetings, managing e-mail and telephone calls, checking your mobile phone for messages, and dealing with interruptive visual and sound alerts from electronics.

**1999:** E-mail had just started to enter the workplace. Your only interruptions were impromptu meetings and telephone calls. Outcome: You focused on your position's responsibilities with minimal disruptions.

# Invite Information In: Improved Focus

**Read, type, talk. Read, type, talk.** Phones, laptops, desktops and tablets allow for great flexibility in communicating, yet these modes of communication can continuously challenge our ability to stay focused and manage tasks efficiently. For many professionals, it's not unheard of to juggle answering e-mail, reading a text, and writing a report all within five minutes: many of us manage multiple communication tasks all day long. The challenge about this multitasking is that we humans are unable to handle more than one communication task at a time; for example, it's impossible to read about one topic and listen about another simultaneously. What exacerbates this endless stream of messaging is the sound and visual alerts from the electronics that surround us. Unfortunately, it's common practice to respond to an e-mail or text during a meeting, stop a task to answer a message, and disrupt a conversation to read a text on your smartphone.

**What's really happening when you're juggling multiple communication tasks?** As stated at the beginning of this book, when we multitask, we increase our error rate by 50 percent. It's not only multitasking that has an adverse impact on our work, but it's also calls and notifications from electronics that challenge us too. In a study by Florida State University, participants were seated in front of a computer and given a task to complete: half of the group were interrupted by their own cell phone with text and calls throughout, and the other half of participants were not interrupted. Those participants who were interrupted with notifications made more mistakes throughout the task than those who didn't. In fact, the increase in the probability of making a mistake was more than three times greater for those who received notifications.

**We even interrupt ourselves!** Another challenge with this sophisticated brain is our inability to focus for extended periods of time. The human brain has a limited attentional capacity to deal with large amounts of information. We naturally interrupt our focus often by switching tasks: for example, reading an e-mail for 30 seconds, sipping a glass of water, or looking at the clock. Here are ways to improve juggling communication tasks.

## • Accessing Information Wisely

**A less stressful day.** Continuously checking your e-mail inbox and phone for messages hinders productivity, which can have an impact on your mental health. Unfortunately, we can become addicted to checking messages (see T.H.I.N.K.). According to research, you'll experience a less stressful day if you access e-mail periodically throughout the day. How often should you open the inbox? It's recommended to access e-mail 3-5 times daily, as well as read and respond to messages in batches during these times.

**Set boundaries?** Yes! It's certainly easy to write, *don't read work e-mail after 6 p.m.*; however, many professionals now communicate with colleagues around the world and around the clock. Therefore, set boundaries that make sense for you and your team. For example, essential e-mail is to be sent only during business hours, 9 a.m. to 5 p.m.

## • Benefiting from a Focused Work Life

**How to stay focused.** Even though you'll always be interrupted by telephone calls and co-workers, there's a simple way to ensure you're not unnecessarily interrupted by electronics. Shutting off the sound and visual alerts on a mobile phone and computer will help keep you from being distracted during the business day. Additional research shows that working in a "non-alert status" mode has positive results, which are as follows:

*You'll think smarter.* Multiple studies on managing electronic interruptions as you work have found that you can experience a reduction in intelligence and memory from the breaks in focus. Working without visual and sound alerts support your ability to focus better and improve decision-making.

*You'll feel less stressed.* In a study focused on interruptions and e-mail, the research found that interrupted workers performed faster. However, when people are constantly interrupted, they develop a mode of working faster (and writing less) to compensate for the time they know they will lose when interrupted. Working faster with interruptions has its own cost: people who worked in conditions where interruptions are the norm experienced a greater workload, more stress, higher frustration, and more time pressure. Working without interruptions from electronics translates to less stress and frustration.

***You'll prioritize better.*** According to behavioral economist George Lowenstein of Carnegie Mellon University, "We pay a lot of attention to the most recent information, discounting what came earlier." In other words, with the excessive number of messages we receive, we often give the greatest attention to the message that "just came in," rather than the most important. Shutting off alerts allows you to focus on your tasks according to *importance* rather than the *latest issue*.

**Less is more satisfying.** Yes, it bears repeating! If you're communicating with e-mail for essential purposes, rather than "conversing," you should be receiving less e-mail. In addition, accessing your e-mail inbox less frequently will result in more productive, satisfying work.

**Special Note:** Does working in an alert-free office sound impossible? It's not difficult to implement when everyone is in agreement to improve the office's atmosphere. How nice it would be to no longer hear dings, dongs, and bings every few seconds.

**T.H.I.N.K. More in an
alert-free work zone!**

# T.H.I.N.K. MORE

## Addiction to E-mail and Texting

**Really?** As we learned in the introduction, we are constantly seeking to be rewarded (the caveperson seeks gratification). What "treats of technology" satisfy our need to be rewarded? It's the visual and sound alerts from our mobile phones and computers. According to MIT media scholar Judith Donath, alerts from our electronics offer a social, sexual, or professional opportunity: we receive a mini-reward when answering these messages. These rewards serve as jolts of energy that recharge the compulsion engine, much like the feeling of excitement a gambler receives as a new card hits the table.

Behavior psychologist Susan Weinschenk explains this further based on research by neuropsychologists Kent C. Berridge and Terry E. Robinson at the University of Michigan. According to their research, the human brain has two systems that complement one another and fuel this need to be rewarded. Dopamine causes you to want, desire, and seek: this "wanting" system keeps you motivated to move through the world, learn, and survive. The "liking" system, the opioid, makes you feel satisfied and pause your seeking.

According to Dr. Weinschenk, reading e-mail and checking phones for messages feed our curiosity of wanting and seeking (dopamine system). Yet, responding to and sending messages feed our desire to feel satisfied (opioid system). "It becomes harder and harder to stop looking at e-mail, stop texting, or stop checking your cell phone to see if you have a message or a new text."

# T.H.I.N.K. – Note
## Scenario 4: The NEXT BIG Idea

**Today:** Your boss has just given you the project of a lifetime. The company is launching a new line of basketball shoes, and your boss wants you to develop shoes based on the ideas and demands of seven top athletes. With each athlete, you'll be meeting in his or her respective city, enjoying a game, and conducting an interview during dinner. After your amazing trip, you have pages of notes to review. As you review your typed notes, you realize the athletes all complain about hot, sweaty feet, which makes you draw the conclusion that a more breathable material is the concept the research team should develop. You type a marketing brief, which includes your idea for a breathable fabric. The design team agrees with you and develops a high-tech fabric that will be featured in the new shoes. The new line of basketball shoes debut with a commercial featuring all of the athletes. Sales are moderate. Good job.

**1999:** Your boss has just given you the project of a lifetime. The company is launching a new line of basketball shoes, and your boss wants you to develop shoes based on the ideas and demands of seven top athletes. With each athlete, you'll be meeting in his or her respective city, enjoying a game, and conducting an interview during dinner. After your amazing trip, you have pages of handwritten notes to review. As you read, you grab a pencil and a pad of paper and use mapping skills to help you brainstorm. It works! You realize there is one common concern the athletes share: each player complains about hot, sweaty feet. With your mapping notes, you compose a marketing brief, which includes developing shoes with breathable fabric and a unique idea to cool the bottom of the foot. The design team agrees with you and develops two new technologies: a high-tech fabric that's breathable and an innovative cooling innersole. The new line of basketball shoes debut with a commercial featuring all seven athletes. Sales are tremendous. Orders for the entire line of shoes are coming in every day. Many celebrities are contacting the company and demanding the shoes. What's the best part of the experience? You've become good friends with all of the athletes, and you're being promoted. Congratulations!

### Brainstorming Today versus 1999

**Today:** Laptops make note-taking a breeze, especially if you're a fast typist.

**1999:** Notes were often written by hand with pen or pencil and paper. If necessary, these notes were recorded in type.

## Note: Greater Creativity and Memory

**Got one!** The moment we have an idea, we often find ourselves sitting in front of the screen and hitting the keys on the keyboard, while we think and type and think and type. What we could be missing is the opportunity to create and solve more, as we did when we were in elementary school. Little did we know, all those crayons and handwriting lessons were actually quite good for us, especially for the brain. Read on!

**Doodling is good for you!**

### • Strengthening Your Amazing Memory

**Write is right!** Believe it or not, handwriting with an instrument improves our memory and the ability to conceptualize. Rather than typing notes or ideas, grasp your pen, pencil, or stylus and handwrite your notes and ideas on paper or screen. Two research studies prove why writing is better for your memory and creativity.

**More complex motor functions.** When writing by hand, you use strokes to create letters, rather than selecting a whole letter by touching a key. Virginia Berninger, a professor of psychology at the University of Washington, says these finger movements activate large regions of the brain involved in thinking, memory, and language. Handwriting helps you retain information more effectively than keyboarding because writing by hand involves more complex motor functions.

**More brain power.** A study with college students at the UCLA Anderson School of Management broke students into two groups: one group took notes by hand, and the other group took notes by laptop. Though both groups performed equally well answering questions on recalling facts from the lecture, students who took notes by hand performed significantly higher on conceptual questions than those who took notes using a laptop. It appears the pen is mightier than the laptop!

**Pen, pencil, or stylus?** Whether you're preparing for a meeting, telephone call, or composing an e-mail, letter, report, or manuscript; it's best to handwrite an outline first. You can use paper, whiteboard, or a computer screen, as long as you are writing by hand.

## • Exploring and Expanding Your Creativity

**Get more creative.** Studies suggest that when you use your dominant hand to write, you're not tapping into both sides of your brain's amazing creativity. Take advantage of your creative side by writing with your non-dominant hand. Your handwriting may be poor, yet the ideas that are derived from the exercise can be extraordinary.

**Doodling is good for you.** Who'd ever believe that those illustrations you may have created during a meeting on the handout or in a notebook would prove that you're actually engaged and focused. Furthermore, those doodles may have even had an impact on your creativity. How can this be? According to Sunni Brown, author of *The Doodle Revolution*, as you doodle, you're uniting different neural pathways in your brain, which opens your mind to greater insights, better information, and higher levels of concentration. In a study, participants who doodled retained 29 percent more information than non-doodlers. How? Doodling aided in their concentration by reducing the individual's capacity to daydream or switch to the mind-wandering mode (you'll learn more about this mode in Chapter 3).

**Doodling and creativity.** Benefits of doodling include increased creativity, because you're liberating your mind from traditional linear and linguistic thinking and moving into a more organic thinking space, heightened information processing, heightened information retention, and the ability to view content from a variety of different angles. Who doodles? Many presidents, inventors, and authors doodle. Because each one of us is highly capable of creativity, we can experience the benefits of doodling, even if our doodle is a dog wearing rollerblades, a snowflake, or a simple cat.

# T.H.I.N.K. – Kindness
## Scenario 5: The Staff Meeting

**Today:** It's Monday morning, and you're waiting for your boss to arrive at the weekly staff meeting in the conference room. As you wait, everyone (including you) is busy answering e-mails or texting. Once your boss walks into the room, she opens her computer, launches the agenda document, and begins to review each topic. When she asks about the project you were assigned last week to organize, you quickly inform her that the team was unable to complete the assignment on time. Your group missed the deadline because only two of the five team members responded to your e-mail. You don't mention that one member's response was simply, "THIS JOB IS DUMB!" Your boss asks the team why they were unable to finish the project. Suddenly, her mobile phone rings and vibrates loudly on the conference table. She looks down to view the caller ID, answers the call, and walks out of the room. Everyone returns to reading e-mail and text messages. When she returns three minutes later, she asks the question again. Three team members look up from their laptops, and one person asks her to repeat the question. She asks for the third time, and two colleagues say they don't remember receiving the e-mail request from you. The boss then asks for the assignment to be completed by the end of the day. Your entire team is not going to lunch today.

**1999:** It's Monday morning, and you're waiting for your boss to arrive at the weekly staff meeting in the conference room. You're talking with several people in your department regarding last week's team project, which you were assigned to organize. Once your boss arrives, she begins reviewing each topic on a printed agenda. When she asks about the assignment, you provide her with an update, and each team member adds his or her point as well. She praises the team for accomplishing the project in a timely manner. With such good results, she takes the team to a company-paid lunch. Yum!

**Business Etiquette in 1999 versus Today**

**1999:** Mobile phones and laptops were not commonplace in the office, and you'd never bring your heavy desktop to a meeting.

**Today:** Who doesn't have a mobile phone or laptop?

# Kindness: Better Business Relationships

**Flash and ding.** We are surrounded by electronics that flash text and project sounds to capture our attention. It's not surprising that many of us believe our mobile phones and computers demand more attention than a human being! Though some of the following ideas for managing electronics sound like good common sense, it's not unexpected when not-so-smart or rude behavior is exhibited during the business day.

## • Boosting Business Etiquette

**Leave the electronics at the door.** As you know, the main objective of a meeting is to share information in the development of ideas and solutions. During a meeting, external interruptions from electronics are not only rude; they are costly. According to a survey, two of three users will interrupt a group meeting to communicate with someone else digitally (e.g., via mobile phone or computer). Demand everyone's full attention and end the meeting earlier by requesting electronics be left at their desk. Bring a laptop only if it's needed for presentation purposes. If notes are necessary, write them on a pad of paper or a white/chalkboard. As you've already learned, writing helps you memorize, and it's healthy for your brain too. Furthermore, reviewing the notes with all attendees at the end of the meeting ensures everyone is in agreement regarding next steps and improves the retention rate of the topic(s) discussed.

**Rrrring.** Ringtones are a fantastic way to alert us that someone is requesting our attention. The ringtones available today are endless. A few good ones are an old-fashioned telephone ring, "Happy" by Pharrell Williams, or a Star Wars favorite, "Chewbacca's Yell." The only challenge with ringtones is how disruptive and annoying these sounds can be at the office. To improve your focus and, if applicable, the focus of those around you, turn your mobile phone ring on low and vibrate during office hours.

**The call you must take.** When you must take a call during a conversation or meeting, you should always be polite. For conversations, kindly excuse yourself and be brief. In a meeting, inform the meeting organizer that you are expecting a call. Place your mobile phone in a discrete place on vibrate (pocket or on the side of your seat), and when the phone vibrates, excuse yourself, and walk out of the room. By doing so, you're less disruptive to colleagues. Some attendees may think you're just going to the restroom.

# ONE LAST NOTE

**Special note to management.** Professionals in leadership roles who expect employees to carry their mobile phones or laptops with them for messaging purposes are supporting an inefficient and unhealthy business environment. On average, electronic interruptions cost employers one hour of lost productivity per day per employee. The ability of team members to stay focused throughout the day is essential for their health, relationships, and quality of work.

# Chapter 2

# The E-mail Diet: Gaining Time and Integrity

**Your mind on e-mail.** What's really happening to you when you're reading and responding to multiple e-mails? Is it simply all business? The answer may surprise you. Many of us read and respond to our messages in batches. With each message, a different emotion, a different reaction, and a different response. This arduous task of managing a multitude of replies and retaining information has an impact on our emotional intelligence. What is emotional intelligence? It's our ability to recognize, understand, and manage emotions. When we feel stressed, the areas of the mind that respond to fear take over, which weaken our ability to use our brain parts that help us make rational choices or reason logically. If you feel overwhelmed and anxious as you manage e-mail, these negative emotions will have an impact on how you respond to each message. Subsequently, poorly managed communication causes stress, which affects your mind, health, and career.

**The "triple whammy" of messaging.** The emotional impact of managing e-mail and text is not the only cost to consider. Electronic messaging also has a tremendous effect on productivity, which has a major impact on our ability to meet day-to-day objectives. Ultimately, this loss of productivity affects the bottom line. Setting aside the emotional impact of messaging, the following is an example of how costly a brief e-mail can be at the office.

**Donuts in the cafeteria!** You've just finished a morning meeting with a group of colleagues, and there is a large box of jelly and chocolate-frosted donuts left over. Of course, your boss doesn't want to see this food go to waste, so he decides to e-mail everyone in the office the following: "Please help yourself to the free donuts in the cafeteria." After the message is sent, you notice that within minutes, three people get up from their desks and walk to the cafeteria. What just happened? The company experienced a costly loss in productivity. However, it's not only due to those who went to get a donut.

**1 Box of Donuts = $180.97**

**How can that be?** It's only a message about some leftover food. The impact of e-mail is greater than we think. Of course, typing and sending a brief e-mail isn't costly. The real expense is the cost of each employee being interrupted by an alert, reading the message, and, for some, responding to it. Every e-mail message, regardless of its content, interrupts an employee's focus, which has an impact on productivity. According to a study conducted by basex and research at the University of

California, Irvine; it can take an employee an average of 5-25 minutes to return to an original task after an interruption. What is the cost of a brief e-mail sent to 50 employees about free donuts in the cafeteria? The estimated cost in work hours/pay is outlined below. The example is based on the *least* amount of time for the employees to return to an original task.

### Cost of an E-mail to 50 Employees

| Action per Employee | | Time/Cost |
|---|---|---|
| Open and read e-mail | | 1 minute |
| Return to task due to interruption | | 5 minutes |
| | **TOTAL** | **6 Minutes** |
| 50 Employees x 6 Minutes | | 5 Hours |
| **Average Pay x Hours = Cost** | | **$137.10** |

**Why does the e-mail's initial cost begin at $137.10?** The average pay for a U.S. private sector employee is $27.42 per hour. If you multiply $27.42 times 5 hours, the cost is $137.10. This cost represents the *first* e-mail sent to all 50 employees: it does not include responses to the message; for example, "trying to cut back" or "thanks." In fact, every e-mail sent in the office has an impact on the bottom line, regardless of its brevity. Imagine if you worked in an organization of 500 employees and a colleague sent a two-page e-mail with incorrect information.

### Cost of a Two-Page E-mail to 500 Employees

| Action per Employee | | Time/Cost |
|---|---|---|
| Open and read e-mail | | 9 minutes |
| Return to task due to interruption | | 5 minutes |
| | **TOTAL** | **14 Minutes** |
| 500 Employees x 14 Minutes | | 116.6 Hours |
| **Average Pay x Hours = Cost** | | **$3,197.17** |

Again, with the average pay for a management employee at $27.42 per hour, the opening cost of this e-mail is $3,197.17. However, the reply-all questions and reissue of the communication will more than double the cost of the initial e-mail.

# Gaining Time and Integrity

**You've got to be a snob.** All too often, professionals choose e-mail as their primary choice when communicating. A thought pops into their head and the *urgency* to communicate supersedes the *effective* way to communicate. The average business professional receives over 120 messages a day (over 30,000 per year), and this number is rising every year. What does this deluge of overwhelming messages represent? Most e-mail messages either substitute for conversation or do not relate to the position's responsibilities. In other

**Be an e-mail snob!**

words, these messages are unnecessary and unproductive. How can we eliminate much of this needless messaging? You've got to become an e-mail snob.

**Demand the Best.** What are you looking for in the e-mail you receive? The answer is simple, everything you need and nothing you don't. How do you receive, send, and post quality information? You become an e-mail snob, an expert in electronic text, and a commander of communication! Yes, put that nose up high. You're too smart to be reading and sending just stuff: you're seeking quality, not quantity. You'll find below helpful ideas that allow you to be more productive, build better business relationships, and secure content. Above all, you'll enjoy working on more important tasks than managing messaging.

## • It's Nothing Personal—It's Business

**With love, Aunt Betty.** If you're receiving e-mail from friends and family at your business address, ask them to send messages to your personal address instead. E-mails from family and friends arriving in your business e-mail inbox can be too distracting; for example, Aunt Betty's recipe for Hungarian goulash shouldn't reside in your business inbox next to a proposal for your largest client. It's smart to keep business and personal e-mails separated. With a "business only" inbox, you can achieve the following:

- Lessen the number of personal interruptions at work
- Keep your personal business, personal
- Ensure company e-mail is strictly business

**Do the same.** In addition, if you're requesting that you receive only business e-mail at your company's address, ensure you're reciprocating the action with family and friends. If friends give you their business e-mail addresses, ask them for their personal addresses instead. What if they question you? Let them know you're looking out for their best interests.

## • Avoid Bits and Pieces Messaging

**Stop communication chaos.** Every day, many of us send or receive two-word or even two-sentence e-mails. As explained, these "bits and pieces" e-mails are costly. There are smarter ways to fend off managing too many messages:

- Pick up the telephone—a brief call can result in a productive conversation
- Write the brief thought down and discuss the issue the next time you meet
- Use cloud-based project software

## • Enjoy a Bit of Spam Each Day

**Billions of marketing messages (spam) are sent every week.** Tell those marketers you're too important for all of the spam they are "serving." If you're receiving too many marketing messages, simply unsubscribe to those companies that are not providing content that you need. If you want to ensure your business e-mail address doesn't receive any spam, set up a separate e-mail account. Therefore, when you receive an important message from your boss, it's not lost amongst 20 marketing messages.

**Why did unsolicited e-mails become spam?** We know that the real SPAM is spiced ham, dating back to the Second World War, which is still available today from Hormel. On the other hand, the spam we receive daily in our e-mail inboxes represent the unsolicited messages from advertisers. Why did unwanted e-mails receive the name "spam"? The answer lies with the British comedy team "Monty Python." Back in the late '60s, a group of wildly humorous British friends created the comedy series, *Monty Python's Flying Circus*. On their television show, they featured a sketch about SPAM; of course, they were referring to the canned precooked meat. The sketch features two customers in a restaurant ordering breakfast. On the menu, SPAM is included with every meal. For example, SPAM and eggs, pancakes and SPAM, coffee and SPAM, and SPAM, SPAM, SPAM, eggs, and SPAM. However, one of the patrons strongly expresses to the waitress that she doesn't want SPAM at all. Hence, the patron's disdain for the unwanted SPAM made the name easily transferable to the unwanted e-mail we receive too often.

## T.H.I.N.K. MORE

### An Internet Diet Too?

**Yes!** You've learned the dopamine system keeps you seeking and wanting and the opioid system makes you feel pleasure. Of course, there's more. The dopamine system is stronger than the opioid; therefore, you seek more than you're gratified. When you're on the Internet searching for information, reading news, or shopping; your dopamine system is in full throttle resulting in a dopamine-induced loop. Overall, you feel rewarded from seeking, resulting in you seeking more! The unpredictability of the Internet, from ads to e-mail messages, also stimulates the dopamine system. This system is especially sensitive to "cues" that a reward is coming. Small rewards like visual and sound cues enhance the addictive effect. The outcome of too much stimulation can result in exhaustion, and the constant switching of attention makes it difficult to accomplish tasks.

## • The Wonders of the Virtual Conference

**Avoiding endless e-mail questions.** You have information that contains several key points that you must communicate to your team that lives 2,000 miles away. If the communication is highly important and open to misinterpretation, use the power of virtual conferencing to relay your information. The advantages are numerous: (1) interact in real time, (2) hear tone, (3) view body language, and (4) present essential visuals. After the meeting, if necessary, send a follow-up e-mail or letter to attendees to reiterate the objectives of the meeting.

## • Say Goodbye to the Distribution List

**The power of posting!** Millions of professionals are on an ever-expanding number of e-mail distribution lists. From reports to newsletters, the volume is increasing daily. Because we receive these updates in our inboxes every day or week, they add to the growing number of e-mails we should not send through messaging. Again, posting documents on an internal site:

- Lessens breach of proprietary, confidential information
- Decreases the number of unnecessary e-mails
- Reduces needless interruptions

**Work smart!** Post daily, weekly, and monthly updates, such as reports, employee newsletters, and meeting notes. When a post is new and requires an announcement, use the strength of e-mail to announce the new posting.

## • Threads Can Get You Ahead

**Who isn't guilty of this mishap?** You return to the office after a few days on vacation. You take a deep breath and launch your e-mail. How wonderful, you only have 256 messages to read. You begin the arduous process of answering messages. You respond to a message by selecting "reply all" and proudly state to everyone who received the e-mail, "We've never done that before." Moments later, you find that a colleague had responded to everyone on the same e-mail two days ago, "Yes, we did that type of work last year." You not only made a buffoon of yourself by responding three days later, but you also provided the wrong information. Yikes!

**Organize electronic mail wisely.** To ensure you're not creating unnecessary messages, organize your inbox by subject or "thread." You'll alleviate opening and closing of the same subject e-mails and avoid recalling a message.

**T.H.I.N.K.** Imagine if you, your team, or even your entire company decided to change the manner in which you managed electronic communication and adhered to the guidelines of T.H.I.N.K. The need to review threads of information will no longer be necessary!

## • Tell Them You Don't Need It

**Sorry, I don't need that information.** It's not just external e-mail you've got to control; it's internal as well. According to research, 61 percent of the e-mail you receive is nonessential to your position. Imagine how wonderful the office would be if the only communication you received was information that enhanced your job. To reduce unnecessary messaging, discuss with your colleagues a plan for distributing information.

**Oops!** In regard to e-mail you shouldn't have received, according to a survey by a U.S. staffing firm, nearly 8 out of 10 advertising and marketing executives confessed they've made a mistake sending an e-mail to the wrong recipient. Here are some examples:

- An e-mail regarding confidential salary information was sent to the entire company
- A job offer was sent to the wrong candidate
- A message about restroom etiquette was accidentally sent to a client

## • Carbon Copy, Not Constant Communication

**CC or Not CC?** Too many of us are over CC'd with e-mails. It appears to the sender that if we have *anything to do* with the content, we should be copied. Ugh! How do you determine whether someone should be CC'd on a particular subject? Just ask! Again, discuss with team members, especially your boss, how information is to be distributed.

**What does CC represent?** For some of you, you know the abbreviation originated many years ago. Before e-mail or copiers, if you were indirectly associated with the subject matter of a paper letter or interoffice memo, your name was listed under "cc" on the bottom of the document, which meant you received a "carbon copy" of the correspondence. What's a carbon copy? It's ugly. To make a copy of a letter or memo, you'd place a carbon sheet between two pieces of paper and place them into a manual typewriter. The imprint from the typewriter keys onto the top paper caused the pigment from the carbon to imprint on the second piece of paper. If you had a typo, you'd have to erase on both pages—it was awful! With such an involved process, you'd only send letters and copies when absolutely necessary. You can understand why "putting it in writing" was rarely the way professionals communicated.

## • Smart Software Tools for Collaboration

**Let's collaborate online.** Cloud-based communication and project management tools are ideal for quick, in-the-moment collaboration among team members. Using these tools has many advantages:

- Reduces use of traditional e-mail
- Allows for real-time file sharing
- Improves task/workflow management
- Offers 24/7 remote access
- Provides search options of data

In addition, the advantage of these collaborative programs is that they often prompt invaluable voice or video conferences!

**Everyone is onboard.** Though collaborative software offers internal messaging specific to a team's needs, messaging is still another form of electronic text. Following the guidelines of T.H.I.N.K. is smart business when using these programs.

## • Thank you!

**You're not welcome.** Yes, this statement seems a bit harsh, yet too many e-mails are simple "thank you" responses that clutter e-mail inboxes. Think twice before you send, thank you!

## • So, Did You Hear the One About . . .

**Now for a joke.** Dave, an insurance agent, enters the home of a potential client, John. Dave sits down on a chair where John's dog, Ralph, is lying underneath. Dave begins talking about a life insurance policy and soon realizes he has bad gas from the burrito he ate for lunch. The first time Dave breaks wind, John yells at his dog, "Ralph!" Dave is relieved that his potential client believes it's the dog that has gas. The second time Dave breaks wind, John yells again, "Ralph!" The third time Dave expels gas, and it's a doozy, John gets up and yells, "Ralph, get out from underneath that chair before that man poops on you!"

**There's nothing like a good joke.** A quick laugh about life's mishaps is fabulous. Though, there are good reasons why jokes are best shared with colleagues at the water cooler and not through e-mail. As you've read, e-mail has a "hidden cost": each message does have an impact on the business day. Additionally, sending a joke you may think is humorous may not be humorous to someone else.

## Smart Communication Management

**How to send what.** As reviewed, selecting the appropriate way to share and distribute your communication has a great impact on your health, productivity, and interpersonal relationships. When information requires documentation, the following guidelines provide smart and effective ways to communicate.

# How to Send What

**Send internal e-mail for the following:**
- Meeting confirmations
- New postings

**Post internal documents on a secure site:**
- Daily/weekly/monthly/annual reports
- Corporate/department announcements
- Proposed or final plans/meeting notes/action plans
- Policies and formal updates
- Research documents
- Executive team directives
- Corporate announcements
- Employee benefit information
- Employee newsletters

**Send non-confidential e-mail to clients and vendors:**
- Announcements (press)
- Meeting confirmations
- Marketing and sales information
- Quotes/Invoices

**Post external documents on a secure site:**
- Proposed or final plans/meeting notes/action plans
- Agreements

**Mail confidential interoffice paper memorandums:**
- Board correspondence
- Performance, disciplinary, compensation matters

**Mail or present confidential, external communication:**
- Introductions
- Formal next steps
- Confirmation of agreements (contracts)
- Presentations

# Chapter 3

# The A.R.T. in Great Business Writing

*i* is the marketing genius of Apple Computer. The Apple marketing team named many key products based on the human life experience, which is 100 percent first person. Every one of us can identify with the powerful word of *i* or *I*: it's simply how each of us perceives the universe. What's the greatest challenge about our *I* world in our never-ending exchange of information? Whether we are conversing with another person, reading an e-mail, or thumbing a text, we think *I* and *me*. However, at the same time, our listeners and readers are also thinking *I* and *me*. This challenging exchange is one of the reasons why communication is often such a complex process. It's like shoveling sand against the tide: it's really hard to do.

*I* **is better when we're talking.** Overall, our *I* world is easier to manage when we are conversing with someone: tone is heard clearly, and miscommunication can be easily corrected.

41

Though, when words are expressed through black text on screen or paper, miscommunication increases dramatically. Misread tone, misinterpretation, and poor composition skills contribute to the many challenges we experience in the exchange of information in the written form. As we all know, understanding how to write well is essential for every business professional. A great tool to use as a guide to improve your communication of ideas, thoughts, and facts can be found in the simple, yet powerful acronym A.R.T. Before we learn about the A.R.T. in great business writing, let's review the amazing attentional system of the human brain, which will provide you with greater insight into the composition process.

**Where was I?** Do you ever find yourself reading a letter or memo and suddenly stop to realize you never really absorbed the content? Where were you? During those moments, your brain was in its natural state, the "mind-wandering mode." In his book, *The Organized Mind*, Daniel J. Levitin, psychologist and neuroscientist, explains that the brain has a four-circuit human attentional system. This system works to help you think, dream, and pay attention. Your brain's attentional system comprises four components: (1) mind-wandering network, (2) central executive network, (3) attentional switch, and (4) attentional filter. Understanding how these modes work together will help you in the thought process of creating and writing. First, let's focus on the two dominant modes of our attentional system, which are the mind-wandering and central executive networks.

**A mind at rest.** When your brain is in the *mind-wandering mode*, it's at rest and in its natural state. In this state, you're daydreaming, where your thoughts turn inward. For instance, you think about what you'll have for lunch or imagine yourself winning an award. However, this daydreaming state is powerful and can lead you to greater creativity and solutions. Have you ever taken a shower or gone for a walk and resolved a nagging issue? During those moments of what appears to be mindless shampooing or walking, you were actually experiencing the mind-wandering mode. This brain state is marked by the flow of connections among disparate ideas and thoughts, and a relative lack of barriers between senses and concepts, all of which allowed you the opportunity to resolve an issue or realize a new idea.

**A mind focused.** What's the opposite of the mind-wandering mode? It's when you're giving all your attention to your boss's speech or walking in an unfamiliar area. This mode is the *central executive*, which keeps you focused and on task. The central executive network works hard to keep you from being distracted when you're engaged in a task. In this mode, your thoughts are both inward and outward.

**Switching back and forth.** Almost all of the time, your brain is either in its mind-wandering or central executive mode. When one is mode is active, the other is not. These two modes switch back and forth all day. A great example of this switching is when you're composing and typing a report or e-mail. During this on-task mode, you find yourself typing quickly because you have many thoughts to express. Then, you stop. Your mind drifts and your thoughts go inward. You start daydreaming about the great dinner you enjoyed the night before. What has happened? You've just experienced switching from the central executive mode to the mind-wandering mode. Another example of switching between modes is when you're in a long meeting. At the onset of the conference, you're often attentive, yet after 10 minutes or less, you may find yourself daydreaming about a vacation you recently took with your friends. Why does this happen so easily? The answer lies with the fact that the mind-wandering mode is more powerful than the central executive mode. When we become bored while in a meeting, reading, or managing a routine task, we switch to the brain's natural state of the mind-wandering mode.

**The big switch.** How are you able to go from the mind-wandering mode to the central executive mode? You have an *attentional switch* that allows you to go back and forth between these two modes. This switch enables you to shift from task to task, such as solving an issue in one minute and answering a colleague's question moments later. However, too many switches can make you tired or even dizzy.

**The person walking down the hall.** The final part of the attentional system explains why we are often so easily interrupted. The fourth component of this system is the *attentional filter*. Whether your brain is in the mind-wandering or central executive mode, your attentional filter is almost always active. Therefore, when you're reading a report at your desk and notice someone walk by from the corner of your eye, it's your attentional filter doing its job. This filter's key responsibility is to keep you aware to ensure you are safe and out of danger.

**Your brain at work.** As you've read, our thought process is highly complex. When you're composing, you want to create and solve in the mind-wandering mode, yet you require your central executive mode to write and type. Understanding when you need quality thinking time for solutions or creativity, versus task time for writing and typing, is essential in the composition process.

**Your brain and A.R.T.** Now that you've grasped an understanding of the attentional system, let's couple this knowledge with ideas for developing well-written works. What is the first step in improving your composition skills?

The answer is to consider yourself as an artist. You may not be Monet, Rembrandt, or Picasso, but your e-mails, memorandums, letters, and reports are works of art with A.R.T.

## Using A.R.T. to Your Advantage

**Writing is a work of art, even in business.** As you've read, composing well-written communication involves our extraordinary thought process, which includes the two dominant modes of the attentional system. During this great thought and creativity, you're an artist when you compose: the canvas is your paper or screen, and your brush is a pen, pencil, stylus, or keyboard. With deep thought and strokes of an instrument, you create works of art for the audience. Cleverly, the word "art" not only represents the end result of each composition, but it also represents a great acronym for the creative process of composing. Using A.R.T. as a guide when writing e-mails, texts, letters, and reports can help you produce works that are mutually beneficial for you and your reader.

**What does A.R.T. represent?** This hard-working acronym stands for the words that support well-written composition, which are Attention, Relevance, and Takeaway. Almost all writing, with the exception of personal journals, is intended for another's eyes. Therefore, creating works that capture Attention, provide Relevance, and deliver a Takeaway include the elements of effective communication. A great example of a direct mail "work of art" is the Publishers Clearing House mailer. It's got it all. Attention, Relevance, and a Takeaway are embedded in this one-of-a-kind direct mail piece; of course, we'd all like the Takeaway of $7 million a year for life!

**Be smart and use A.R.T.** Regardless of the type of communication you're sending, whether it's an e-mail, one-page letter, or a 20-page report; the elements of good writing include A.R.T. Let's read more about what this acronym represents and how it can support the improvement of your composition skills.

# A is for Attention

**What's the secret of the first five minutes of a feature film?** Great directors know they must capture your attention quickly at the onset of the movie to keep you interested. Here are more examples of directors who were able to keep viewers' attention: in *Titanic*, Jack Dawson wins his ticket and in Disney/Pixar's *Toy Story*, the toys come alive, every child's dream. Whether it's a movie, advertisement, or a business letter, the first few moments are the key to the audience. Why? As we learned in the opening of this book, our dopamine system keeps us seeking and wanting during the waking hours of the day. If an element captures our attention and interests us, we become satisfied thanks to our opioid system. Therefore, how you capture your reader's attention at the opening of a letter, e-mail, or report is essential in the composition process, because we are striving to entice our reader to seek and read further.

**You're a writer!** You may not be James Cameron writing his next screenplay, but you are a writer inspiring your reader to seek and be satisfied. How can you capture your reader's attention? Begin your correspondence with one or more of the following:

- Include a greeting
- Open with the main reason for the message
- Provide a benefit and feature
- State an interesting fact or ask a question

In the following examples, the *italicized* text demonstrates how you can capture the reader's attention.

### Example 1: Meeting invitation

Dear Pat, Corey, and Preston,

*Once more, congratulations on your excellent contributions to the Patriot Project.* You'll find a memo attached to this invitation from the President of our division thanking you for your efforts. Let's meet for a company-paid lunch on Wednesday at the Simon Pearce Restaurant.

Sincerely,

Suzanne

### Example 2: Client E-mail

Good morning Greg,

*Thank you for your order.* As we discussed, the delivery date for the shipment is now June 21. The shipment will also include the 25 boxes of paper you requested this morning.

Kind regards,

Adam

### Example 3: External Partner E-mail

Dear Julia,

*Your help is appreciated.* Please call me when you have a moment to discuss the Jenkins account. Let's review the following topics:

- New representative introduction
- Marketing plan
- Meeting time

Thank you,

Logan

# T.H.I.N.K. MORE

## WHAT was THAT?

**Wow!** Why do some things capture our attention and others don't? Each day, we make choices of what we allow to access our thoughts and capture our attention. For instance, you're walking through the grocery store and the sign above a cookie display reads, *FREE cookies with purchase of milk*. For most of us, we're easily attracted to the word *free*: it's the idea of getting something for nothing. This word is also one of the most eye-catching terms in the English language. Obviously, we are attracted to more than words. There are four overarching characteristics of things that enthrall us, which are as follows:

• **You're fascinated by other people.** The human experience is, simply, human. We enjoy learning about one another, our past, and our future. We like reading and watching about fictional and nonfictional characters. It's not surprising that the best-selling magazines are about people.

• **Your feelings of fear and hope are front and center!** Our center of emotion, the amygdala, is easily stimulated. A great example is an evening news program. It often begins with major concerns affecting our world (fear), yet ends on a positive note, which can be a human interest story (hope).

• **You enjoy patterns and repetition.** Why do you like watching soccer, football, or baseball, or listening to music? For sporting events, you're intrigued by the predictability of the game and the surprising twists and turns, such as an interception during a football game. For music, it's the repeated beats, melodies, and lyrical phrases that interest us.

• **You're intrigued by open-ended questions.** We like to search for answers. Open-ended questions entice us to think, make connections, and learn. Here's an example: What did you enjoy about reading this section?

**Oh, no!**

**One last word on capturing attention by comparing humans to goldfish.** Here's another interesting bit of information as to why it's important to "hook" your reader at the beginning of your work. The human attention span has shrunk. According to the National Center for Biotechnology Information, U.S. National Library of Medicine, the average attention span has dropped from 12 seconds in 2000 to 8 seconds in 2013. Eek! Furthermore, a goldfish has a slightly better attention span at 9 seconds. Again, get your hook out early to capture your reader!

# R is for Relevance

**How do they do it?** *People* Magazine knows how to do it, as well as hundreds of other magazines and newspapers. What is it? The editors and journalists of these publications understand how to not only capture attention, but also create Relevance for their stories. Of course, the writers at the *National Enquirer* are exceptionally good at capturing attention and developing relevant content, whether these eye-catching stories are true or not! For all periodicals, editors and journalists are paid to know what articles most readers will find important, which then prompts their consumers to open their wallets and buy. However, journalists are not the only ones who can develop relevant content for their readers: savvy businesspeople know how to craft the well-written word too. So, what is the key to relevant business writing? As we learned at the opening of this chapter, we think *I* and *me*; therefore, we must alter our viewpoint and think *you*.

**What do readers want to read?** In regard to composition, you've probably heard the following concept: you write as if you're in the reader's shoes. With that said, how can you compose as if you're the reader? You accomplish this often challenging task by applying two key concepts:

- Replacing the pronoun "I" with "you"
- Building importance with the reader's viewpoint

**Seek and satisfy.** By applying these concepts, you create Relevance for your content. As you know, the main objective of corresponding is to get your point across, yet to do so in a manner that keeps your reader seeking (dopamine) and satisfied (opioid) with information that is clear and purposeful. Let's begin with the first concept: applying the *you* pronouns in your works.

**Replacing the pronoun *I* with *you*.** All too often, we receive messages and letters that include sentences such as "I am sending you . . . ," "I've attached the . . . ," or "I want to tell you . . . ." Did you notice something similar in those sentences? It's the pronoun *I*. The challenge with using the *I* pronoun too often in business correspondence is it clearly states the content is written from the writer's perspective, rather than the reader's point of view. What can using *I* too much in your writing be similar to? You may come across to your reader as sounding a bit adolescent. A humorous example of this type of communication appears in the classic movie *Caddyshack*. In the movie, the spoiled teenager, Spaulding, and his grandfather, Judge Smails, are walking from the golf course to the club restaurant. As they walk, Spaulding whines, "I want a hamburger. No, a cheeseburger. I want a hot dog. I want a milkshake." His grandfather sternly remarks, "You'll get nothing and like it."

**No one wants to be like Spaulding!** You can easily alter your communication by replacing the pronouns *I* and *we* with the pronouns *you* and *your*. In each example, compare the sentences below. Which sentence do you prefer?

### Example 1

A. I've posted the June shipment report.

B. You'll find the June shipment report has been posted.

### Example 2

A. Can we meet at 2 p.m. in Conference Room B?

B. Are you available to meet at 2 p.m. in Conference Room B?

### Example 3

A. I think the idea is fantastic!

B. Chris, your idea is fantastic!

**Did you choose B?** By changing the pronoun in the sentence from *I/we* to *you/your*, you're also changing the viewpoint of the content considerably. Let's expand on this further for composing overall.

**Building importance.** How can you build importance for your message? In addition to using *you* and *your* pronouns, there are two additional ways to create works your readers will want to read. Your communication provides Relevance for the reader when it's written from his or her perspective by considering the following:

- What information the reader believes is most important
- How the content will benefit or not benefit him, her, or them

**What does this mean to me?** When you read, you're always seeking what impact the information will have on you. Of course, your reader is seeking the same. Whether you're the boss or colleague, creating well-written correspondence from the *you* viewpoint informs the reader about how the communication will affect him or her.

In the following examples, all of the A versions are written in the *I* viewpoint, and all of the B versions are written in the *you* viewpoint. Which version do you prefer, A or B?

### Example 1: Meeting Invitation

### Version A

TO: Joan Corby
FROM: Toni McCluskie
RE: Product Meeting
I am holding a meeting regarding Chocolate Fruits in Conference Room B on Thursday, June 22, from 9 to 10 a.m. Please call me at Ext. 222 to confirm your attendance.

### Version B

TO: Joan Corby
FROM: Toni McCluskie
RE: Your Opinion Matters for Our New Candy Line
Hi Joan,
Your opinion matters to us. You're invited to participate in a taste test and learn more about our new product line, Chocolate Fruits. The meeting is on Thursday, June 22, from 9 to 10 a.m. in Conference Room B. Please call me at Ext. 222 to confirm your attendance. See you there!

**Which meeting invitation would you like to receive?** In Version A, Toni is focused on her own actions, rather than on how the meeting will impact and benefit Joan, which is clearly represented in Version B. Again, when you adjust the viewpoint, the communication becomes mutually beneficial for you and your reader.

### Example 2: New Employee Announcement

### Version A

TO: All Employees
I am pleased to announce Harrison Johnson has accepted the position of Vice President of Sales for the Apparel Division. I hired Harrison for his 25 years of experience in the apparel industry . . . .

### Version B

TO: All Team Members
Please join me in welcoming Harrison Johnson to our company as the Vice President of Sales for the Apparel Division. You'll soon experience the positive impact of Harrison's 25 years in the apparel industry with the launch of our new website dedicated to . . . .

**Does Version A seem all too familiar?** This example is the most common type of announcement sent within an organization. In this version, the executive is stating to the employees what is happening. In Version B, the executive is inviting his employees to welcome the new vice president, and he is also explaining how the new hire will impact the company.

**Which thank you letter do you prefer?** In the next example, the owner of a marketing firm is sending a follow-up thank you letter to the vice president of an apparel company. Which letter would you send?

### Example 3: Thank You

**Version A**

Dear Tom,

I would like to take a moment to thank you for your time. I enjoyed meeting with you and your staff. I want you to know how happy I am that you're considering my firm to design the catalogs for the fall clothing line, and I believe you'll find us easy to work with.

Also, I understand your concern regarding the cost. I can guarantee that we will stay within budget and deliver a brilliant brochure. I will call you next week to discuss the proposal. I hope you have a great weekend.

Sincerely,

Jill

**Version B**

Dear Tom,

You were right about the results of the basketball game. Our team is having such a great season. Again, thank you for meeting with us last Tuesday. Considering our firm as the design team for your fall clothing line is greatly appreciated.

Throughout the design process, you'll find our staff to be professional and competent. Your concern regarding cost will be taken into serious consideration every step of the way. You have our guarantee that your company will send its customers a brilliant brochure.

Tom, as you suggested, we will discuss the proposal further next week. Enjoy your weekend.

Sincerely,

Jill

**Big difference!** In Version A, Tom is inundated with Jill's *I* perspective. Though Jill was polite and expressed the value of hiring her company, her message focuses primarily on her viewpoint. On the other hand, in Version B, Jill's message builds Relevance by considering how the content will impact and benefit Tom's apparel company. Furthermore, the message opens with a sentence that captures Tom's Attention.

We've reviewed examples that provide positive news, let's review an example delivering bad news.

### Example 4: New Opportunity

### Version A (e-mail message)

Dear Eric,

Please allow this e-mail to confirm that we will no longer be the management team for the Jones Corporation as of April 2065. I did all I could to keep Justin from ending the contract. The competition offered his company something, and I can't seem to figure it out. Hey, the guy was a bit of a jerk. I will set up a meeting to discuss a plan to win his business back, as well as seek an opportunity with the Jones' competitor, Creedon & Litchfield Company.

Best regards,

Cindy

### Version B (meeting invitation)

Dear Eric,

Thank you for your time and positive thoughts during our conversation regarding the Jones account. As we agreed, Justin's decision to hire another firm is disappointing. Let's meet and prepare to win this account back, as well as seek an opportunity with the Jones' competitor, Creedon &

Litchfield Company. In addition, for your review, a sales strategy is attached to this invitation to prepare for the upcoming meeting.

Best regards,

Cindy

**The Bs have it!** Hands down, Version B is the better of the two. Did you notice? In all the B versions, the word *I* was not present in any of the sentences. You'll often find that correspondence written with the *you* viewpoint is easier to read and a more effective means of communicating.

**IMPORTANT:** We are now interrupting this chapter for an important message. When the content includes information the reader will find disappointing (unless it's a simple order that cannot be filled), it's best to contact the person(s) directly to discuss. If necessary, send a message to confirm the conversation.

# T is for Takeaway

**What do you want me to do?** Now that you understand the importance of grasping Attention and building Relevance, the third key element of A.R.T. is the "Takeaway." With every message we receive, there is one important question we must know: what do you want me to do? Again, when we receive a message, we immediately seek (dopamine) its purpose. Providing your reader with the action item for your communication, especially at the opening of your message, helps ensure you'll meet the objective(s) of your e-mail or letter. In the following examples, which version do you find provides a better "Takeaway"?

**Example 1: Great sales**

**Version A**

TO: Al
FROM: Fred
RE: Great Sales

I can't believe how great sales are! I want to start planning on increasing inventory levels over the next six months to make way for the same fantastic holiday season we had last year. Can you believe David doesn't think we can keep this momentum? I know consumers will love this new product! I believe we are going to open up more channels of distribution over the coming weeks.

I want to increase inventory levels ASAP. Do you think Duncan Smith can help? Do you have his telephone number?

**Version B**

TO: Al
FROM: Fred
RE: Request—Contact Information for Duncan Smith
Hi Al,

Your advice would be greatly appreciated. Our sales have been fantastic and to keep the momentum, we'd like your opinion. I heard Duncan Smith was instrumental in improving operations at Squirrel Inc. Do you believe with his experience, he could support my organization's growth? If so, would you please forward his contact information? As you know, we are planning to increase inventory levels over the next six months in preparation for another outstanding holiday season.

Appreciate your help,

Fred

**Where's the Takeaway?** In Version A, Fred focuses on his *I* viewpoint throughout the message, and he leaves his request of Al at the end of the e-mail. In Version B, Fred composed a message with Al's viewpoint and included the Takeaway at the beginning of the message.

### Example 2: Employee parking

### Version A

TO: All Employees
RE: Do Not Park in Unauthorized Parking
It has come to my attention that many employees are parking in unauthorized parking spaces throughout the complex. I've received calls from our fellow business neighbors complaining about this issue. Even the owner of the building has called me to complain. I can assure you that your vehicle will be towed at your expense if you park in the unauthorized spaces.

### Version B

TO: All Employees
RE: Special Message on Parking at Our Offices
Please park your vehicle in our company's designated parking spaces. As you know, we lease this space from Corby Management. The company has informed us that they will begin towing vehicles parked in unauthorized spaces. Unfortunately, if your vehicle is towed, you will be responsible for the cost. Please call James Walsh if you have any further questions. Thank you.

**Eek!** Version A will certainly capture the attention of the employees, and it easily communicates how rude the boss is. Version B is written with the *you* viewpoint, yet it's firm about the consequences for not following company parking guidelines.

# Using Your A.R.T.

**The amazing creative process of writing.** A.R.T. supports you with the power to compose with thoughtfulness and skill. You own the opportunity to introduce your reader to new information with flair. As you've read, in developing your works, you use the mind-wandering mode to brainstorm ideas, yet rely on your central executive mode to execute. What's a great idea for ensuring you apply A.R.T. to all your works? As you draft, write A.R.T. at the top of the page. You may find it to be a helpful tool to guide you in your quest to create works that will engage and satisfy your reader. Overall, in the process of composition, you're relying on the most sophisticated machine on planet Earth—your amazing brain.

# Chapter 4

## Selling Yourself: Get Readers to Buy You

**H**ello! Welcome to the chapter that provides concepts to help you interest readers to buy you. What is meant by "buy you"? As you know, whenever you're sending a communication, regardless of the content, the writing represents you. Because the objective of composing is to ensure your reader understands you, you are indeed seeking to enlist him or her to buy your ideas, thoughts, solutions, directives, etc. In this chapter, you'll review ideas that support you in composing works that keep your readers reading.

### • Award Yourself with a Happy Mindset
**What's the key to successful writing?** It's ensuring you're in a positive state of mind when composing. You'll be amazed how a good attitude, especially when you're conveying not-so-good news, impacts your ability to compose well. Are you looking for an example as to why it's important to have a positive

mindset? Think back to the last time you were frustrated by a message that made you sigh and roll your eyes. For many of us, quickly clicking the Reply button, tapping on the keyboard, and hitting Send resulted in communicating a message that you wish you never sent. Avoid the "why did I do that" and allow yourself the opportunity to respond in a positive frame of mind.

**Seeking to change your mood at the office?** As you learned in the last chapter, placing yourself in the mind-wandering mode is advantageous. How do you lead yourself to this natural state of mind? Here are ideas that may help guide you to a happy and thought-provoking frame of mind for composing, generating ideas, preparing for a meeting, and more!

**Listen to your favorite music.** Place your headphones on and listen to one or several of your favorite songs. Research has proven that the power of listening to your favorite songs, regardless if your music taste is country, rock 'n roll,  or classical, will help place your mode of thinking in the mind-wandering state.

**Go for a walk.** Another way to clear your mind and boost your brainpower is by going for a walk. The human body was made to move and exercise. What's happening as you exercise? Your blood starts moving, which brings energy to your brain from glucose and oxygen. Walk on!

**Read a few inspirational quotes or jokes.** Reading uplifting content is a good way to stimulate a happy mind. Here are some examples:

"Believe you can and you're halfway there." Theodore Roosevelt

"Whoever is happy will make others happy too." Anne Frank

"Be a rainbow in someone else's cloud." Maya Angelou

**Buy a colleague a cup of coffee.** Do a good deed. Helping others is good for you. Here's an even better idea: ask a colleague to join you for a walk to the local coffee shop. Imagine the power you'll have to create when you return.

**Meditate.** Take a moment to relax, reflect, and breathe. Meditating can increase memory and creativity and decrease anxiety.

**Must you always be happy for critical thinking?** The answer depends on you. Thinking in a negative mind-set can help you conceptualize, analyze, and evaluate. In this state of mind, you are often more skeptical and less gullible. For example, think about the last time you felt challenged, which resulted in a great idea. What will spark your next opportunity? Will it be a negative or positive mood?

**Special note:** Are we always happy in the mind-wandering state? Unfortunately, the answer is *no*. Our minds wander over 30 percent of the time; and for some of us, our minds can wander up to 50 percent of the day. The goal is to place yourself into a happy mindset that is *focused* on completing a specific task at hand.

## • Did You Mention My Name?

**A great book.** According to Dale Carnegie's *How to Win Friends and Influence People*, the sweetest sound to a person's ear is his or her name. In addition, each one of us also enjoys seeing our name in writing too. Consider the many products that feature names on them, from mugs to towels. Therefore, for a communication sent to five people or less, ensure you include names of the recipients at the beginning of the message. For correspondence addressed to one person, if there's an opportunity to state the person's name again within the message, such as the closing, please do so.

## • Respecting Your Reader's Interest

**Huh?** Reflect on the last message you read that was a true challenge to understand what the writer was asking of you. In most cases, the action item was at the bottom of the message, and the writer droned on about subject matter that didn't pertain to you. As mentioned in the last chapter, when we read, we are seeking information and want to know its purpose. Why are we receiving this message? What am I supposed to do? Therefore, for every communication you write, place the reason(s) for the message within the first paragraph. You're not only providing your readers with key information at the onset, but you're also respecting their time with the option to read further and improving their ability to comprehend your message.

**Why is it important to place it up front?** The simple reality about reading is we don't pay attention to boring stuff. As mentioned in the last chapter, when we become bored, our mind switches to the mind-wandering mode (daydreaming). Looking for an example? The following is a memorandum sent from a CEO to his entire staff regarding a new employee purchase program. To protect you from absolute boredom, the example below is written as a short story.

**GO-UP! Corporation**

Charlie is the CEO of a company that manufactures innovative, energy efficient new vehicles, "GO-UP" carplanes. These new electrical vehicles can easily be driven around the neighborhood or flown high in the sky. Employees love working for the company, and everyone has expressed an interest in purchasing a GO-UP vehicle. Charlie realizes he must address his employees' demand now that the carplane will begin entering the marketplace in less than a year. With a high demand of the vehicle worldwide, Charlie knows he must stagger his employees' requests. He types an e-mail that will be sent to all employees. The first eight paragraphs of his lengthy message explain his dream of building the company, the challenges in developing the production model, and the demand for the vehicle from celebrities to politicians. In the ninth paragraph, at the bottom of page 3, the CEO finally explains the new employee purchase program.

**Who read the CEO's memorandum?** Only a handful of employees read the entire communication, wherein the final paragraph, they learn the CEO will be raffling off one "GO-UP" carplane at the end of each month for an employee to purchase at cost. Because Charlie's memorandum was titled, "Employee Purchase Program," he should have explained the specifics of the employee purchase program at the beginning of the message. Once again, a well-written communication respects the reader by placing the reason for the communication at the opening of the message.

## • Getting Everyone in Agreement

**Selling through smart meetings.** You have an issue or opportunity: it could be implementing a process, announcing an idea, or seeking a solution. What's the best way to sell it; in other words, to get everyone in agreement? Host a meeting. All too often, professionals will send an e-mail with directives without generating input from key stakeholders. By hosting a meeting before you send a directive in a letter or e-mail, you're not only inviting key stakeholders to give their opinion, but you're also finalizing key steps with them.

**Looking to ensure it's a successful meeting?** Here are key elements to consider when preparing to meet with clients, colleagues, and vendors:

- Agenda - provide an agenda with the meeting request
- Concise presentation - keep your attendees' attention
- Snacks - people love to snack
- Joke - open with tasteful humor or a quote
- Write - record key meeting ideas, concerns, etc.
- Action - agree to an action plan

## • Excellent, Great Job!

**Compliment or cash?** Research has proven that giving someone a compliment has the same positive effect as receiving cash. Yes, you just read the word "cash." Complimenting a colleague in writing or verbally is just smart! The power of showing appreciation is said best by Mark Twain who quipped, "I can live two months on a good compliment." Because the people we work with are important to our careers and, at times, our sanity during challenging moments, praising your co-workers on a job well done makes for a happy, healthy, and wise environment. Also, when you compliment someone, you're not only building that person's self-esteem, you're also building your own.

**Compliments should be professional.** Praising a person on his or her physical appearance is not always wise. You'll find below a list of ways to demonstrate your appreciation.

- Managing a challenging issue successfully
- Achieving or exceeding an objective/goal
- Demonstrating determination/initiative
- Using excellent communication skills
- Introducing a new idea or process
- Showing attendance and loyalty (work anniversary)

**Put it in writing.** What's a fantastic way to show your appreciation? Place your words of praise in writing. Receiving a personal note regarding your achievement is the best compliment of all, whether it's sent electronically or on paper. For many of us, we prefer to receive a hand-written message. You may want to invest in notecards!

## • Everything You Need, Nothing You Don't

**Brevity is beautiful, especially in writing.** If you're sending an agenda, action steps, announcement, or a business statement; compose your work with facts and figures, and if possible, in bullet-point form. According to a survey, more than 81 percent of professionals strongly dislike e-mails that are too lengthy. Furthermore, only 1 in 10 people read an e-mail in its entirety. Again, it's critical to discuss issues first and create action steps.

**Compare the versions!** You're about to begin reading an e-mail that seriously requires brevity; of course, the abbreviated version follows.

### Version A

Good afternoon Melissa,

I must tell you what happened today. A disheveled woman arrived at our store at approximately 10 a.m. this morning requesting a refund for a dress she had purchased over two weeks ago. Our associate, Ms. Green, asked the customer for the receipt, and the woman screamed at her, "I lost it!" Ms. Green then inspected the stained garment to find the tags were removed, and it smelled like a cat litter box. She informed the customer that we could not accept the garment for a return, because of its condition. At this time, the woman screamed again, "I want to see the manager!" I arrived at the front desk immediately and listened to the customer's complaint.

As I told you, I politely explained to the customer that we could not accept the item for return, because of the already stated reasons. The customer then said she would not leave the store unless we provided her with a credit for the garment. Well, she stood in the store for over two hours. I then had to inform her that if she did not leave, we would have to ask our security officers to escort her out. Of course, I had to ask our officers to do so, and as they walked her out, she screamed obscenities, and she bellowed, "I'm contacting the media about this store!"

Again, I figured if the customer went to the press about this issue, corporate should be informed. Let me know if there is something more we should do.

Best regards,

Matt

**Version B**

Good afternoon Melissa,

Thank you for taking my call regarding the challenging situation we experienced with a customer returning a garment. Please let me know if there is further action necessary. Below is an overview of the incident.

- Customer returned a worn garment without a receipt
- Store management explained the store's refund policy
- Customer would not accept store policy
- Security escorted customer out after two hours
- Customer threatened to contact the media

Kind regards,

Matt

**The facts, please.** In Version A, Matt sent Melissa an e-mail and waited for her response. Unfortunately, when the regional newspaper contacted Melissa, she explained to the journalist that she didn't know about the incident. In B, Matt managed the situation properly by speaking with Melissa first and following up the conversation with an internal post. Melissa was ready to speak about the issue when the journalist called.

# T.H.I.N.K. MORE

## The Key to Selling Your Ideas

**Please repeat.** The key to selling your ideas. When we are introduced to new information, its first entrance into our mind is through our short-term memory. According to the paper titled, "The Magical Number Seven, Plus or Minus Two" authored by Harvard University psychologist George A. Miller, space is limited in the short-term memory of your mind. Miller's research in 1956 provided evidence that the capacity of our short-term memory is seven (plus or minus two). In other words, we are only able to store between five and nine items of information in our short-term memory. Here's a visual: consider your short-term memory to be "empty shelves in a grocery store" and items of information to be "loaves of bread." As you're presented with new items or bread, these shelves fill up quickly. For example, when you're given a seven-digit telephone number, the shelves in your short-term memory fill up fast and hold this information. However, the shelf life of these digits (bread) is only 2-30 seconds. So, if you don't repeat or act on this information within moments, the information is not memorized or the bread goes bad and is thrown out. Therefore, when you're selling your ideas to another, be certain to repeat the information again, and please repeat it again. Don't let your bread go stale!

## • Your Brain on Positive Words

**The strength of words.** Words have the power to influence the way we think. Consider a message you received from a colleague that was both accusatory and rude. The hostile message prompted your eyes to open widely; and soon after, you felt your heart rate increase. Words such as *wrong*, *disappointed*, and *failed*, as well as profane language can disrupt specific genes that play a key part in the production of neurochemicals that protect you from feeling stressed. As humans, we are wired to worry. It's a component of the fight or flight response and is designed to keep us safe. Bad words can release stress-producing hormones and neurotransmitters, which will interrupt your brain from functioning properly. For example, have you ever noticed that you're unable to think clearly when you've received criticism? For most of us, once we hear negative feedback, our brain partially shuts down the logic-and-reasoning centers located in the frontal lobe.

**Be positive.** Your objective as a professional is to communicate with a positive attitude, regardless of the situation. As you're writing or speaking, use positive words that help sell your ideas for solutions or new concepts. Listed below are more than 30 words to choose from.

| | | |
|---|---|---|
| Accept | Great | Quality |
| Accomplish | Guarantee | Recommend |
| Appreciate | Handle | Reliable |
| Benefit | Invite | Respect |
| Best | Kind | Safe |
| Bonus | More | Smart |
| Create | Natural | Tested |
| Excellent | New | Teamwork |

| | | |
|---|---|---|
| Forgive | Premium | Think |
| Free | Proud | Trust |
| Good | Proven | Valuable |

## • Adhere to the Chain of Command

**Attention, please!** The U.S. military is the perfect model of an organization that adheres to the chain of command. For most organizations, adhering to a chain of command or hierarchy of authority is critical in the proper supervision of employees at all levels, from the CEO and down. With e-mail, the chain of command can easily be broken. In the following paragraph, you'll find a common communication challenge many organizations experience.

> Justine was very pleased with her new ideas for managing customer service calls. With great enthusiasm, she decided to send an e-mail to the entire management team, which explained her concepts. As she pressed the Send key with confidence, Justine believed the management team would embrace her ideas, and she would receive accolades for her work. What happened? An hour later, Justine's boss, the manager of customer service, met with Justine and asked her why she would send a message to management without her approval. Justine's smile faded from her face, and she responded, "I thought everyone would be pleased."

**Discuss the office e-mail chain of command.** Messaging has allowed us to communicate with everyone in the office at the press of a key. As stated earlier, speak with your supervisor/manager/director/vice president/big cheese in your organization about how to best manage e-mailing and posting information.

## • Get Your Signature Style!

**Sincerely.** The ending of your communication is as important as the beginning. Create a signature or sign-off that represents you. Good examples are as follows: *best regards, cordially, kind regards, sincerely, thank you*, and *sincerely yours*. Remember to keep it professional. Business correspondence is not the place for cute, overly casual greetings and sign-offs.

# Chapter 5

# How to Avoid Sounding Like a Jerk

**J**osh, Brock, and the big apple pie order. At 6:30 a.m., Josh walked through the office doors of The Big Organic Restaurant corporate headquarters. He's so proud to work at such a fantastic company that operates 176 restaurants, which serve only organic appetizers, entrees, and desserts. After his morning meeting with his boss Brock, Josh was thrilled that Brock asked him to place organic pie orders with local bakeries for the restaurants. Brock instructed Josh to order pies with fruits that are in season and e-mail copies of the orders to his attention. After spending three hours

The Big Organic Restaurant

placing orders with local bakeries, Josh proudly clicked the Send button and sent copies of the orders to Brock.

**What happened next?** Brock responded quickly to Josh's e-mail and demanded the order of 6,150 apple pies be reduced immediately. The e-mail ended with the statement, "What were you thinking? I don't know if I can trust you ordering for the restaurants." After Josh had read the e-mail, he was greatly disappointed; his face became flushed. He then returned a quick response to Brock's e-mail and explained that apples are in season, and the price of these pies was extremely low. After Josh had reduced the order of apple pies to 3,075; he left for an early lunch with a colleague. When Josh returned to the office, he found it difficult to focus on his position's responsibilities.

**Your brain and negative, negative, negative.** Why was Josh unable to think clearly for the remainder of the day? Unfortunately, Josh temporarily lost his ability to concentrate. As explained in the last chapter, for many of us, when we receive negative feedback, the logic-and-reasoning centers in our frontal lobe temporarily shut down. What's happening? In our brains, we have a fear center, our amygdala* (*pronounced um-MIG-duh-luh*). When we experience a threat, this almond-shaped center releases stress-producing hormones and neurotransmitters, which interrupt our brain from functioning properly. For Josh, Brock's e-mail response was too harsh, resulting in Josh's inability to concentrate. *Please note: the amygdala plays a key role in processing all of our emotions, including fear and pleasure.

**We are built for survival.** The most challenging aspect of the human experience is that our brains are wired for fear. Why? Over thousands of years, our brains became hard-wired to protect us from major threats, such as being eaten by a tiger, lion, or bear (oh my). Today, we don't have to worry about being eaten; however, the brain is unable to "shut off" this element of fear. The reality is we focus on survival first and happiness second. The greatest challenge with our fear-centered brain is it continually brings up negative emotions, worries, and past mistakes. How do we manage to communicate not-so-good information with a brain that feeds on negative emotions? By doing so wisely. One of the wonderful aspects of the human experience is our ability to overcome challenges. You'll find outlined on the following pages ways to relay not-so-good information and ensure you're not considered "a jerk."

## • Your Voice is More Powerful than Text

**You have good and bad news to tell your boss, colleague, or client.** What's best? Choose the power of your vocal cords. Again, conversation is always the best choice, because the tone of your voice will never be heard in text on a screen or a piece of paper. For example, in the business story of the apple pie order, if Brock had spoken with Josh rather than sending a disappointing e-mail, Brock would have found that Josh was proud of his work in reducing the company's dessert costs. Brock would have thanked Josh for his work and explained why the apple pie order should have been cut in half. Josh would have adjusted the order and gone back to work.

## • The Emotional, Knee-Jerk Response

**The impulsive oops e-mail.** Our messaging today has empowered us with the ability to provide responses to issues within minutes. Due to this "messaging mania," we are now conditioned to give a quick decision, rather than a more thought-out response. For many professionals, this "knee-jerk response" can result in a decision they quickly regret. As we all know, a well-thought-out response shared at a later time is always wiser than a statement that must be retracted. Again, keep in mind, avoid allowing the *urgency* to communicate supersede the *effective* way to communicate.

## • Public Shaming at the Office—OUCH!

**Ugh!** Imagine if you received an e-mail from your boss that stated the truth: you did not meet your position's responsibilities on a particular issue. Your boss explained what you did not accomplish and made clear the actions you are to take to improve. What was worse than receiving this information in an e-mail? Your boss cc'd everyone on the team! Ugh! If you must provide feedback to a colleague, do so graciously and avoid delivering the message in an e-mail. Enough said.

## • Did You See that E-mail?

**How often do you hear that statement within a week?** Be cautious about placing negative information in e-mail, especially those not-so-nice comments that are better left "untyped." Unfortunately, these unprofessional messages can always be forwarded. What did your parents always say? If you can't say something nice, then don't say it at all. Here's a good example of an "oops e-mail": this story is true.

**A CEO's mistake.** Two travelers wrote to an airline to complain about their less-than-stellar travel experience and requested compensation for a delayed flight and missed concert. They were not satisfied with the air carrier's offer of $200 in vouchers; subsequently, they sent an e-mail to the company's communication manager explaining they wanted more for their troubles. Their e-mail was then forwarded to the company's CEO. Apparently, the CEO didn't think the passengers had any right to complain, so he sent a harsh response via e-mail to his communications manager, Pasquale. The only problem was the CEO accidentally selected "Reply All," and the passengers received the e-mail too. The e-mail read as follows:

> "Please respond, Pasquale, but we owe him nothing as far as I'm concerned. Let him tell the world how bad we are. He's never flown us before anyway and will be back when we save him a penny."

## • Give Me the Bad News First

**Bad news and good news.** What would you prefer? According to a study, when faced with receiving both good news and bad news, 78 percent of people preferred to receive the bad news first and then the good news. In the study, participants were divided into two groups: one group was told they were *receiving* good and bad news, and the second group was told they were *delivering* good and bad news. Those receiving the news preferred the bad news first. However, study participants delivering the news were split on what to manage first: some participants preferred to give the good news first. Generally speaking, if 78 percent of people prefer to receive the bad news first, you're smart to adhere to the research!

## • Dealing with a Bad Performance Review?

**The challenging conversation.** For employee performance reviews, the concept of bad news first, good news second changes. If you plan on providing your employee with feedback

to improve, you're wise to relay the good news first. Why? In a study, participants were provided feedback: some participants received the bad feedback first, while others received the bad feedback last. All of the participants were also given an opportunity to improve their behavior through a video program or assist the experimenter with a remedial task of stapling packets. Surprisingly, those participants who received the bad news first were less interested in changing their poor behavior and chose to help the experimenter with a task. Those participants who received the bad news last chose to improve their behavior and opted to watch a video to improve.

## • Putting the Bad News in Writing

**Give it to me first!** Now that you understand the reasons for providing bad news first, let's review some examples when you must deliver bad news in writing.

### Example 1: Customer Service

### Version A - *avoid*

Dear Valued Customer,
Please call a service representative at 1-800-555-NUMBER regarding your recent order. Due to low inventory, we are unable to ship the item you requested, the J.T. Polo Man shirt in Red.

### Version B - *recommended*

Dear Shaun,
Please accept our apology. We are unable to ship the item you requested, the J.T. Polo Shirt in Red. We can send you the same shirt in Pink or Green. You're welcome to call a client representative at 800-555-NUMBER or e-mail client services.

### Example 2: Design Revision

### Version A - *avoid*
David,
Would you be available to meet us again to discuss the web design? Does Tuesday work for you? We understand your time is valuable and will pay your fee to redesign several of the web pages you provided last week. Unfortunately, due to poor communication with our marketing team, several of the pages you designed did not meet with our brand objectives for the launch of the new website. We require a redesign immediately.

**Version B -** *recommended*

Good morning David,
You'll find a voice mail message from me on your phone. In short, thank you for delivering the excellent web designs so quickly. Though, due to creative differences within our team, several web pages require a redesign. We will compensate you for the additional work. Please call me to set a meeting. We look forward to talking with you regarding next steps.

### Example 3: Encouragement

**Version A -** *avoid*

Cameron,
Dude, you need some good news. I was surprised to hear that after all your work, you lost the Timberlake account. I can't believe they decided to hire the Chelsea Group—of all agencies. You're just not having a good month.

**Version B -** *recommended*

Hi Cameron,
For the past several months, you've worked diligently on the Timberlake account. The account's decision to sign with the Chelsea Group was surprising. Your good attitude and strong sales acumen will soon bring a great opportunity your way.

# T.H.I.N.K. MORE

## Why "No" is Bad for You and Business

**Oh, yes!** Saying the word "no" not only has a negative effect on your listener, but also has a negative effect on you. In the book, *Words Can Change Your Brain*, the authors, Andrew Newberg, M.D. and Mark Robert Waldman, explain that even viewing this word for less than a second increases activity in your amygdala (fear center). Yes, this word can release dozens of stress-producing hormones and neurotransmitters, which interrupt the normal functioning of your brain. So, what do you do if you must relay bad information? For each negative expression you convey to your reader or listener, it's recommended that you generate three to five positive messages. Therefore, for reading that negative word twice in this paragraph, here are positive words for your brain: you're so smart, you're hardworking; and most importantly, you're a pleasure to work with!

## • "But" Can be Negative

**Ensure it's a compliment.** Have you ever received a compliment that didn't sound like words of praise? Chances are the word *but* may have been included in the intended kind words. Sometimes, using the word *but* in words of praise can convey a negative message. In the examples below, Sentence A conveys a slightly negative tone, yet Sentence B conveys a more positive tone.

**Example 1: Idea**

A. I agree with your idea, but I need more time
   to consider it.
B. Please give me a little time to consider your idea:
   it's an interesting suggestion.

**Example 2: New Website**

A. The website design is great, *but* the opening message needs some work.

B. Let's discuss a slight revision of the opening message on the outstanding website you've created.

## • Ugly versus Pretty Words

**You have the choice.** In circumstances when you're communicating a message your reader may find disappointing, you possess the power to alter the content. In other words, you can express yourself using a more positive approach. For example, avoid using negative words such as *can't, don't, not, won't,* and of course, *no.* Review the examples below, which would you prefer to receive?

| Negative | Positive |
|---|---|
| We can't meet today. | We can meet tomorrow. |
| I don't agree with you. | I differ in opinion. |
| No, we will be in Chicago | Sorry, we will be in Chicago. |
| The computer is not for you. | The computer is for Lesley. |

## • If You Must Say No, Just Say So

**Don't be vague.** There are times when we must provide our listener or reader with information that will not be well received. Seek to provide him, her, or them with a response that is direct and clear. Also, use A.R.T. as your guide when you're composing the message. In the following examples, you'll find Version B to be more polite and direct.

## Example 1: Internal Communication

### Version A - *avoid (e-mail)*

Harold,

I reviewed your idea for shipping samples directly to our sales force from the factory. I'm not sure it will work. Thanks for the input.

### Version B - *recommended (telephone call)*

Hi Harold,

Your suggestion to ship samples to our sales force from the factory is an interesting concept. The only concern is ensuring that each representative receives the correct sample line. Without a company representative at the factory, it's difficult to ensure proper distribution. Therefore, we will continue to ship from our corporate offices. Again, thank you for the suggestion and keep them coming!

## Example 2: External Communication

### Version A - *avoid*

Steve,

According to company policy, I'm not sure I'm allowed to send those files to you.

### Version B - *recommended*

Dear Steve,

Thank you for your message. Because the document you're requesting is proprietary information, at this time, I am unable to provide you a copy. If the status changes, a copy will be sent to you immediately.

Kind regards,

Lauren

### • **Your Face and Ears Turned RED**

**What?** You've just read a message directed at you that was not only negatively charged with emotion, but also contained incorrect statements. Worst of all, your boss received a copy of the message too. How do you manage a message full of rubbish? Instead of responding to the message with an e-mail, speak directly with the person who sent the message and with your boss. Resolution rarely comes from messages bouncing back and forth between professionals. In addition, this information is documentation, which can be saved and, worse, forwarded. Conversation is always best—use it wisely!

# ONE LAST NOTE

**Too much!** It's not surprising to receive messages that are "negatively charged." As stated earlier, we receive an overwhelming number of messages on a daily basis, which equates to over 25,000 per year. What was it like in the '70s? With little technology at the office, the average executive received approximately 1,000 communications per year. When voice mail entered the office, the messages elevated to 4,000 annually. With the introduction of e-mail in the '90s, the average number of communications received increased to 8,000 per year. Not just executives, professionals receive an average of 120 e-mails daily, not to mention the text messages we manage around the clock from our smartphones. It's not surprising that many of us "go a bit bonkers," responding to message after message! Let's T.H.I.N.K. more.

# Chapter 6

# What Secretaries Don't Want You to Know

**W**hen did the modern office come to life? Surprisingly, the answer lies with the American railway system. The office came to life when railroads began to expand across our nation. Almost all businesses in the early 1800s were local: merchants oversaw their businesses themselves. With the expansion of the railroad, the demand to employ hundreds of employees across miles of land launched the necessity for the modern-day office. To properly manage the American railroad, a new system of organization was required, which included a vast interoffice communication and management system. The birth of the business office came to life with all of its glory from paper clips to politics.

**The old days of the secretary.** Let's catapult from the 1800s to 1980s.

Before the personal computer entered the business world, the typing of documents at the office was the responsibility of the secretary or administrative assistant. Many large organizations implemented "typing pools," which were designated areas within the office where secretaries focused primarily on the editing and typing documents for the management team and executives of the company. Obviously, with the introduction of the personal computer, many professionals began typing their own correspondence, which drastically reduced the number of typists needed in the workplace.

**Take a memo.** The days of the boss saying to a secretary, "take a memo," are long behind us. Now, the administrative tasks of managing communication are upon us all. What's the challenge with this situation? Many professionals have never participated in a business communications or an administrative assistant class. This chapter is dedicated to providing you with the tools to enhance your own administrative responsibilities when necessary.

## Ideas Secretaries Don't Want You to Know

### • The Big 3

**It started when you were young.** Do you remember sitting in elementary school listening to your teacher explain how to compose? Learning how to write was reinforced through each year of school we attended. Of course, organizing a report on the rivers of America is slightly different than drafting a business letter. For both, your information must be organized by key points with supporting facts. The essential element of the business letter is that it represents and supports your organization.

**The power of parts.** For business correspondence, secretaries were schooled in the organization of thoughts, ideas, and facts. They learned business messages include three key parts, which are an *opening*, a *body*, and a *closing*. To ensure your reader is able to assimilate

your communication easily, apply these three parts when you're composing. Each part has a distinct purpose, which is as follows:

**Part 1.** The *opening* of an e-mail, letter, or memo is the opportunity for you to convey to your reader the purpose of the communication. It's also where you have the greatest opportunity to interest your reader by capturing his or her Attention and stating the Takeaway of your communication.

**Part 2.** The *body* of your correspondence is where you further explain the reason you're communicating, which is accomplished through sequenced paragraphs or a paragraph with supporting details. Here, you continue to support the Relevance of your message. The body can be one bold sentence or 20 paragraphs outlining a new concept.

**Part 3.** In most instances, the *closing* of your e-mail, letter, or memo is the easiest part of writing. You provide an overview, restate your Takeaway, and express appreciation.

**Example**

Hi Ashley,

*Opening*

Thank you for inquiring about the new Run, Run, Run Athletic Shoe. This technologically advanced shoe will be available in April at specialty retailers and on our website, where you'll learn about a great opportunity to save!

*Body*

You'll love running in the new Run, Run, Run Athletic Shoe. The shoe conforms to your foot, and the material of the midsole provides superior support. The breathable fabric of the shoe keeps your feet comfortable and dry for a jaunt down the street or a 10k run.

*Closing*

We'd love to hear about your experience with the new running shoes and will award you $25 off your next purchase. Simply post your thoughts on our website. We look forward to hearing from you!

Best regards,

The Run, Run, Run, Running Team

## • Where You Put What

**It's about organization.** Years ago, most business letters were created by a boss dictating a message to a secretary. As the boss dictated, the secretary wrote the message in shorthand and translated it later. Secretaries organized, typed, and distributed communication from short memorandums to long letters. A key element of this task was the ability to know *where to put what*; in other words, how to best organize and sequence the information within the correspondence. What did the clever secretary do? Administrative professionals organized the content strategically with the proper placement of the *main point*.

**Placement is key.** Where you place the main point of your communication within the document has an impact on how the reader assimilates the text. What is the main point? It's the primary reason you're communicating. For example, if you're requesting a three-week vacation, do you place the request (main point) at the opening, body, or closing? The following examples explain the difference in the placement of the main point through three similar letters.

**You're going on vacation!** Your rich aunt and uncle have invited you to join them on a three-week vacation to Australia: they are paying for the entire trip, including an outback safari. Unfortunately, you only have two weeks of paid time off, and a three-week vacation request must be approved by a

**Sydney, Australia**

vice president. To convince your boss to approve the vacation, you've got to persuade her. In the following versions, which memo would you post in your employee file? Please note: the main point appears in *italics* in each version.

**Version A.** You've chosen to state the main point in the *opening* of your correspondence and provide supporting details in the body and the closing. This approach is the most common in composition.

Dear Boss,

Thank you for sharing your interesting story about Tasmania. As we discussed, this letter outlines my vacation plans. *My request is for a three-week vacation, August 1-21.* You'll find below an overview addressing any concerns you may have.

According to our HR Department, I am entitled to ten of the fifteen days requested; however, I understand compensation will not be provided for five of these days. In addition, company policy states vacation time longer than ten days must be approved by a vice president. Therefore, upon your approval, a request form will be forwarded to Jim Studds.

You'll find the responsibilities of my position will be met by working Saturday mornings from 7 a.m. to 1 p.m. for the next few weeks. After speaking with Larry, June, and Gary about this vacation, they have agreed to manage my responsibilities during my absence.

Your approval is greatly appreciated.

Best regards,

*Your name here*

**Version B.** The main point is placed in the *body* of the correspondence. Using this approach, you inform the reader with supporting details that ascend to the main point and descend with additional details. This type of communication is great when you're leading your reader through subject matter for sales and marketing letters.

Dear Boss,

Thank you for sharing your interesting story about Tasmania. As we discussed, this letter outlines my vacation plans. You'll find below an overview addressing any concerns you may have.

In regard to your inquiry about extended vacation time, according to our HR Department, I am entitled to ten of the fifteen days requested; however, I understand compensation will not be provided for five of these days. In addition, company policy states vacation time longer than ten days must be approved by a vice president. Therefore, upon your approval, a request form will be forwarded to Jim Studds. Overall, *I am asking you to approve my request for a three-week vacation, August 1-21.*

You'll find the responsibilities of my position will be met by working Saturday mornings from 7 a.m. to 1 p.m. for the next few weeks. After speaking with Larry, June, and Gary about this vacation, they have agreed to manage my responsibilities during my absence.

Your approval is greatly appreciated.

Best regards,

*Your name here*

**Version C.** By placing the main point in the *closing*, you're providing your reader with all of the supporting details leading up to the main point. This approach is good for special requests, announcements, scientific explanations with a surprising outcome, and of course, sales and marketing letters.

Dear Boss,

Thank you for sharing your interesting story about Tasmania. As we discussed, this letter outlines my vacation plans. You'll find below an overview addressing any concerns you may have.

According to our HR Department, I am entitled to ten of the fifteen days requested; however, I understand compensation will not be provided for five of these days. In addition, company policy states vacation time longer than ten days must be approved by a vice president. Therefore, upon your approval, a request form will be forwarded to Jim Studds.

You'll find the responsibilities of my position will be met by working Saturday mornings from 7 a.m. to 1 p.m. for the next few weeks. After speaking with Larry, June, and Gary about this vacation, they have agreed to manage my responsibilities during my absence.

*Your approval of my request for a three-week vacation, August 1-21*, would be greatly appreciated.

Best regards,
*Your name here*

**Did you notice the A.R.T. in these versions?** You captured your boss's Attention with *Thank you for sharing your interesting story about Tasmania*. You ensured that the message had Relevance for your boss by stating, *you'll find the responsibilities of* . . . . And, the Takeaway was requesting approval for the extended vacation.

## • Adding Style to Your Writing

**You can be a great designer when composing.** Did you know there are a variety of styles to choose from to add flair to your ideas, thoughts, and facts? Rather than just stating your content, compose works that help in interesting your reader. What styles are available to you? You'll find a sampling of styles below:

| | | |
|---|---|---|
| Feature/Benefit | Level of importance | Procedure |
| Compare/Contrast | Definition | Interest |
| Request/Explain | Timing | Positive/Negative |

**Please show me.** What's the difference between making a statement and making a statement with *style*? Compare versions A and B in the following examples. Which version do you prefer?

**Say it with Style!**

## Example 1: Features Only vs. Features and Benefits

### Version A - *features only*

The new e-mail system, FST EML, will be available to all employees beginning September 1. It will be necessary for everyone to partake in an instructional seminar to learn how to use this new program. Classes will start on July 1. Each department supervisor will be contacted to set up a training class for direct reports by May 15.

### Version B - *features and benefits*

E-mail just got easier for us! The new e-mail system, FST EML, will be available to all employees beginning September 1. FST EML will provide you with an easy-to-understand format, quick-find address system, and accept or decline buttons. To ensure the success of our new system, you'll receive a meeting invitation for a one-hour training session by May 15. Classes will begin on July 1.

**What a difference!** As you know, the reader is always looking for how the content will benefit him or her (building Relevance). Providing your reader with the benefits of a feature demonstrates you're accomplishing this objective.

## Example 2: Statement vs. Compare/Contrast

### Version A - *statement (e-mail)*

I recommend that we hold our national meeting in May at the Redwood Resort in Florida, rather than at the Maine Adirondack Resort. The cost is the same for both.

### Version B - *compare/contrast (meeting invitation)*

Do you prefer Florida or Maine? Should we consider holding our national meeting at the Redwood Resort in

Florida, rather than at the Maine Adirondack Resort? As always, the meeting will take place the first week of May. With the conference in Florida, the weather will be more accommodating for the attendees; as a result, we can also sponsor our annual golf outing. The Maine facility is offering us an extremely reasonable room rate, yet the airfare to Florida is less costly than Maine. Overall, the cost of the meeting is the same whether it's in Florida or Maine. Please accept this meeting invitation to finalize.

**Florida or Maine?** A compare/contrast paragraph makes the text more interesting to read and provides the necessary evidence to support the main point.

### Example 3: Request vs. Request and Explain

#### Version A - *request (e-mail)*

The copier machine has required too much maintenance. I'd like to purchase a new copier for our department. The cost is $650.00, and I believe it's a great price.

#### Version B - *request/explain (meeting invitation)*

It's time to meet about our copier. Over the past several months, the copier machine in our department has required maintenance three times: the total cost was $476.75. The repairperson informed us that the machine would require additional parts within the next three months, which will total approximately $275.00. Because the copier is seven years old, do you agree with me that we should purchase a new one? The cost of a new copier is $650.00. Furthermore, this copier will include additional features, including collating and stapling of documents.

**Explain of course!** Provide your reader with an explanation. You may not want to provide too much information, yet just enough to make an educated decision.

## • Happy Birthday!

**Do you enjoy when someone remembers a special event in your life?** How does it make you feel? Most likely, you appreciate when someone says, "happy birthday." Acknowledging a milestone, anniversary, or birthday helps you build relationships with colleagues and clients. As we learned in Chapter 4, by complimenting others, you're also building your own self-esteem. How? For example, when you recognize colleagues' work anniversaries, you're enhancing your chances of those people liking you. Overall, when you give someone a compliment, you then consider yourself to be a good person; therefore, you build your own self-esteem. As you know, it's important to be well acquainted with the recipient, as well as sincere when recognizing him or her.

## • The Power of the Paper Calendar

**Did you just read the words paper calendar?** Yes, you did. You might be thinking, "I have my electronic calendar. It alerts me when I have an appointment." Why should you use a paper calendar, as well as an electronic one? As you learned, the power of writing information down is beneficial for memorizing and creating. A paper calendar by month provides you with an overview of key dates and space for you to write down your meetings and key objectives, both professional and personal. In particular, a 10" x 16" or 8 1/2" x 11" wire-bound, monthly calendar allows you to view month by month with plenty of room to write your goals and meetings on each date. What else should you do? Write in pencil. It's just easier to erase because life is all about change!

# T.H.I.N.K. MORE

## The Power of Three

**Essentials of correspondence.** As we reviewed at the opening of this book, before e-mail, professionals relied on paper letters and memorandums to communicate, which secretaries typed and distributed. The three key guidelines secretaries followed in developing correspondence were as follows: (1) keep the letter or memorandum to one page, (2) focus on one topic, and (3) organize the message into three parts (open, body, closing). On another note, the power of three also helps with persuasion, which is often the goal of business communication.

In a study conducted by professors Kurt A. Carlson of Georgetown University McDonough School of Business and Suzanne B. Shu of the UCLA Anderson School of Management, they found if you're seeking to persuade, the optimal number is three. Based on their report, "When Three Charms but Four Alarms: Identifying the Optimal Number of Claims in Persuasion Settings," they found the number of positive claims that should be used to produce the most positive impression of a product or service is simply, three. When the fourth claim is introduced, consumers' persuasion knowledge causes them to see all of the claims with skepticism.

## • E-mail Folders are a Waste of Time

**Get your time back.** What is the smartest way to file all of those e-mails you receive? The answer is not to file these messages at all. Those of us who have 20, 50, or even 100 file folders in our personal information manager or e-mail program are working inefficiently. According to IBM research, filing your e-mails is more time-consuming than keeping them all in one folder. In the study, it took users 58 seconds to locate a past e-mail in organized folders, yet the average search time for a file in one big folder only took 17 seconds. IBM research revealed that just using the search function can be much faster than navigating through folders to find old messages. In total, users were wasting more than 20 minutes a day filing e-mail, which equates to more than 1 ½ hours per week.

**KISS.** Do you prefer to organize your e-mail in folders? If your organization chooses to send e-mail than post content, you may want to consider filing these messages with the concept of KISS, which is "Keep it Simple and Smart." Choose a basic folder system with no more than four or five folders. Here's an example:

- Your name (e-mails pertaining to key responsibilities)
- Corporate (company-wide e-mails to all employees)
- Reference (key timelines, instruction)
- My benefits (employee information)

This system allows you to keep your inbox free of too many e-mail messages and spend less time filing.

## • All Work and No Play

**Vacation.** The secretary knew the importance of getting out of the office. Of course, assisting people all day long was often quite tiresome and stressful. Smart professionals understand the importance of a break. Employees who take time off from their positions are often more dedicated, productive, satisfied, and healthier than those who forgo time off. What makes time off even better? Don't access your e-mail or answer your business telephone. Your company has provided you with an opportunity to relax, so take it!

## • Great Reference Books to Own

**Buy!** Enjoy the benefits of great reference books at your fingertips. Here is a list of suggested books that will help you improve your communication skills:

- Dictionary
- Thesaurus
- *The Gregg Reference Manual*
- Vocabulary building books

## • Business Correspondence Know-How

**The more you know.** You can easily select a template to create a letter or memorandum. However, knowing the key elements and spacing requirements means you won't have to rely on an administrative assistant or a template. The following pages depict how to format a letter (Block Style) and memorandum.

**Looking to learn more?** Again, *The Gregg Reference Manual* features a guide to formatting letters, memorandums, reports, and many other documents.

# BUSINESS LETTER

January 2, 2065   *4 returns*


Mr. Michael Cassidy
President
The Brightest Concept Company
111 Main Street
Anytown, DC 00000   *2 returns*

Dear Michael:   *2 returns*

Thank you for accepting a meeting with us on such short notice. We were intrigued by your team's ability to grasp our concepts so easily. The following provides an overview of the details regarding our partnership.   *2 returns*

Project Overview
You'll find an overview of the project and key due dates listed below. Please let me know if there are any concerns.

| February 2 | Concepts due |
| March 5 | Provide feedback on concepts |
| April 2 | Prototype review   *2 returns* |

Our Agreement
As we discussed, the contract is enclosed for your signature. Please sign and return the document to Elaine Jones.   *2 returns*

Michael, we look forward to reviewing initial concepts with you. Please let me know when you'd like to attend a baseball game this coming spring. Go Sox!   *2 returns*

Best regards,   *4 returns*

MaryLou O. Taylor
Vice President   *2 returns*

Enclosure

# INTEROFFICE

# MEMORANDUM

TO:  All Team Members    *2 returns*

FROM:  Ted P. Farguss, HR Director    *2 returns*

DATE:  June 22, 2065    *2 returns*

RE: Updated Vacation Policy: Effective Immediately

*2 returns*

Good news to all team members!    *2 returns*

We've changed our corporate paid time off (PTO) policy. Effective immediately, every team member will receive an additional five days of PTO. This policy update includes full and part-time employees.    *2 returns*

If you've already used your PTO for the year, you're entitled to an additional five days.    *2 returns*

As with all PTO, please request approval from your supervisor. *2 returns*

Enjoy!

# Chapter 7

# iCandy: It's All About How It Looks

**"You look marvelous."** Years ago on *Saturday Night Live*, Billy Crystal portrayed the actor Fernando Lamas in a number of skits titled, "Fernando's Hideaway." Mr. Lamas was known for his Latin lover movie roles in a career that spanned more than 35 years. On *SNL*, at the end of each segment of *Fernando's Hideaway*, Billy Crystal would say, "Remember my friends, it's better to look good than to feel good." What does looking good have to do with communication? One word best defines it, everything! We are a highly visual species: our mind views the world in pictures. Also, we like to see patterns; it helps us assimilate information. Because text can often be viewed as a bit boring, it's best to get your works looking marvelous with a bit of iCandy. Here are ideas to spruce up the look your letters, memos, and e-mails; while keeping these works professional in appearance (format).

## • The Ransom Note

**You're sending business correspondence.** Bold type, all caps, and colored fonts capture attention, yet they may send the wrong message. Use basic fonts such as Helvetica or Times New Roman when corresponding. When is it appropriate to apply all caps? Here are two examples:

- THANK YOU for your excellent work.

- WE REACHED $2 MILLION in SALES!

Special Note: Your company may have a style guide on font usage, logo placement, etc. Speak with your supervisor regarding guidelines.

## • Stop the Blob of Text!

**The power of the paragraph.** You probably receive at least one or two messages a day that are a "blob of text." These e-mails consist of many sentences that are not separated by paragraphs, which make them difficult to read. Use paragraphs to separate your key points or topics throughout all of your letters, memos, and e-mails. A good paragraph:

- Supports the subject of the communication

- Opens with a topic sentence

- Includes additional sentences to support the topic

- Provides a logical flow of content

## • Give Space a Chance

**Is your message brief?** Is it too small to divide into paragraphs? Simply apply a little "eye space." When your message is short in length, double-spacing the text helps make it easier to read. Here's an example:

Hi Kathleen,

Thank you for responding to our advertisement for the

role of vice president of manufacturing. We appreciate your time and interest in applying for the position through our website. In the near future, you'll receive a response from our human resources team.

Best regards,

Bob C. Gilfeather

# T.H.I.N.K. MORE

## Ban Slide Presentations?

**Wise presentations.** According to a former U.S. Defense Secretary, the popular programs that create text and image slide presentations should be banned. He's not alone: two CEOs of major companies in the U.S. do not allow their employees to use slide presentations during meetings. Why? They found when this type of presentation is used, it not only limits discussion, but also allows audience members to shift easily into the mind-wandering mode (daydreaming). As we know, the primary goal of a meeting is to share ideas and discuss next steps. These companies found that not using a slide presentation empowered the speaker and audience to become more engaged with one another. What do they use instead? They use a whiteboard, marker, and necessary charts and graphs as handouts.

## • Paragraph Headlines

**Looking good!** Attract your reader's attention with a great visual—the paragraph header. These subject headers are appealing to the eye and provide the reader with a quick overview of the paragraph's content. The following is an example that you can use for a letter or e-mail.

Dear Cindy,

What a fabulous show! Thank you for inviting Catherine and me to the screening of your new television show, *Decorating Daily*. You asked us to provide you with feedback on the program, and you'll find several suggestions below.

<u>Lawn Care for Men</u>

Why have you decided to choose a segment titled, "Lawn Care for Men"? Yes, lawn care is often the responsibility of men, yet there are plenty of women who care for their lawns too. More than half of Americans live alone, which means there are plenty of females caring for their shrubs, grass, and gardens. We recommend you change the segment to "Days Outdoors."

<u>Contemporary Focus</u>

Many styles of the furniture and fabrics featured were beautiful. However, all of the designs were contemporary. Is it possible for you to also feature traditional styling?

<u>Parting Gifts</u>

Catherine and I were thrilled with the coupons we received for future purchases. We also loved the pillows, fabric swatches, and home cleaning products. You may want to include a daily "grand giveaway" to a participant in the studio audience.

Again, thank you for inviting us. We look forward to receiving tickets for future shows.

Best regards,

Karen

## • Be a Bit More Formal

**You're sending a letter.** You have a letter to send through e-mail. You'd like it to be more presentable than just sending text in an e-mail. What can you do? Format the content into a letter using a Word document, save it as a PDF, and attach the letter to an e-mail. The document will certainly express to your reader(s) that you're communication is of importance.

## • A Photograph is Worth a Thousand Words

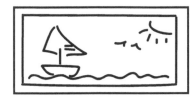

**Seeing is believing.** Allow the power of images to convey your message. When you have the opportunity to include a picture, chart, graph, or graphic; add it to your e-mail, letter, or memorandum. Again, we are highly visual and prefer to see an image rather than text.

## • Front and Center

**Mix it up!** You don't have to place all of the text in a message to the left side of the margin. You can easily highlight a word or words by centering them in the document. See the example below.

Dear Maria,
You've accepted the role of international financial
director for ABC Company.
Congratulations!
We are looking forward to working with you and
your team.

## • Attention, You've Got Bullets!

**Love the list.** Do you have a number of points you'd like to convey to your reader? Apply a list with bullet points: it's easier on the eyes! Compare examples A and B. You'll find example B is easier to read.

### Example A
Please bring the following materials to the sales meeting: laptop computer, marketing binder, recent catalogs, and sales projections.

### Example B
Please bring the following materials to the sales meeting:

- Laptop computer
- Marketing binder
- Catalogs (recent)
- Sales projections

## • Emojis ☺

**Happy!** These icons are great to use when you've established a good working relationship with someone. Avoid overusing these wonderful characters.

# Chapter 8

# Brain, Plus Storming, Equal Ideas

**T**he power of brainstorming. What do the Pyramids of Giza, Ford Model T, and Microsoft Windows all have in common? It's quite elementary. The process for each of these creations began with three key elements: a brain, a writing instrument, and a form of paper. These essential elements in creativity have developed so many of the wonderful and innovative concepts known to man, such as the wireless telephone, office stapler, and skyscraper. Of course, the list of ideas conceived with these elements throughout the centuries is endless. As complex as each one of these breakthroughs was (including the stapler), they were all developed in the human brain, written down on paper, and shared with others. All of these ideas are the results of powerful, successful brainstorming.

**Bringing it all together.** Throughout this book, you've learned ideas on improving the communication process. These ideas have included how your brain thinks, how to develop works for your reader, and the benefits of handwriting. The following paragraphs review elements of these concepts and introduce you to ideas for brainstorming and editing with the overall goal to create first-in-class communication.

## • Peace Out!

**Relax your mind.** You've got a project that must be completed by the end of the business day. You're sitting at your desk and thinking to yourself, "I really need to think." To achieve optimum thinking, you've got to peace out; in other words, get your brain into the mind-wandering mode. As you learned in Chapter 4, the ways to retreat to the mind-wandering mode include the following:

- Listening to your favorite music
- Going for a walk
- Reading a few inspirational quotes or jokes
- Talking with a colleague
- Meditating

**Composition and aromatherapy?** Another way to relax before you compose is with your nose. Studies have shown that it's not only lavender you can use to relax; smelling citrus may help too. Citrus aromas are often useful in curbing stress and anxiety, as well as helping with digestion and nausea. Because we are all different, you may want to experiment with various citrus scents to find the one that has a positive effect on you.

## • Write in the Morning

**When is it best to brainstorm?** Your brain is working at its peak performance in the morning, because creative activity is highest during and immediately after sleep. As the day unfolds, analytical parts of the brain become more active. For most, the morning is the best time to think of solutions, create, and compose. As the day goes on, just like our body, our brain slows down. If you must send a communication later in the afternoon or early evening, take a moment to relax before you compose. In doing so, you're building energy to improve your focus and thought process for composing.

**Need extra help?** If you're challenged with a particular problem and cannot come up with a solution—consider sleeping on it. Before you fall asleep, think briefly about the problem. You may find an answer to this challenge when you wake up. How often do you have a great idea in the shower?

## • Who is Your Audience?

**One, two, or twenty?** As you begin the brainstorming process, consider who your audience is (you've probably heard this many times). Are you writing to one person or a large group of people? How much knowledge does your audience have on the topic? Furthermore, you may find applying A.R.T. during the brainstorming process to be helpful. Write A.R.T. on the top of your page, and consider not only the key points you plan to convey, but also how you can capture the reader's Attention, provide Relevance, and deliver a Takeaway.

## • Pencil and Paper, Please

**Which style do you prefer?** You're about to begin a new work of A.R.T. In developing your communication, do you have a brainstorming style you prefer? Before you begin to compose, identify the style of formatting you'll use while brainstorming. The three most popular are listed below.

- Create a list
- Use index cards and write a different thought on each
- Apply the mapping method on paper or whiteboard

**Special Note:** Avoid organizing your thoughts on paper or screen during the brainstorming process. Simply enjoy writing them down. Keep in mind, if you're seeking additional brainpower, use your non-dominant hand to write, which allows you to tap into more creativity.

## • Leave No Stone Unturned

**Think, think, and think.** Write everything down that comes to your mind. Even if it sounds a bit strange, you'd be surprised where a thought can lead you. In addition, let your mind wander! As we learned at the beginning of the book, mind-wandering is the natural state of the brain, and it is essential in creative thinking. Researchers at UC Santa Barbara have shown that people whose minds wander more are highly creative and better problem solvers. They are able to work on the task at hand, while simultaneously processing other information and making connections amongst ideas. For instance, you'll find you do some of your best mind-wandering (thinking) when driving or working out. Researchers also found the ability to come in and out of mind-wandering at will is very significant and the hallmark of the most creative people. How often does our mind wander? Again, we spend over 30 percent of our time in the mind-wandering mode.

**Looking to ensure you've got it all?** Support your brainstorming by applying the journalistic approach to writing. Do you remember learning this concept back in elementary school? This approach is not only easy to remember, but it's also quite thorough. Therefore, consider the *who, what, where, when, why,* and *how* while you're thinking and writing. Along with the word A.R.T., you may even want to write these words on your paper to help facilitate more thinking.

## • Organize, Outline, Oh Yeah!

**The rough draft.** You've got it all down: you can't even think of another word that could add value. "Start your engines" and organize your ideas on paper or type them on the screen. Develop your rough draft by focusing on the main point or body of the message first. Because the scope of your communication may change while drafting, you'll want to save the opening and closing of the message to the end. At all costs, avoid punctuating and formatting at this stage of composing. Save this task when the entire draft is complete. Time and again, we rewrite and lose valuable time with "housekeeping."

**Good idea.** If your communication is intended to be sent in an e-mail, create it first in a Word document. There are two good reasons to do so: (1) Word applications offer many tools for editing, and (2) you won't have to worry about accidentally selecting Send before you're finished.

# T.H.I.N.K. MORE

## The Key to Group Brainstorming

**Create more!** What are the challenges with brainstorming as a group? According to two professors at the Kellogg School of Management at Northwestern University, there are good reasons why group brainstorming can be difficult. One reason is that the ideas brought to the table at the onset of the meeting are given more weight than ideas that arrive later in the session. In addition, "shout out" ideas are often disruptive to those participants who are thinking (especially when one is in the mind-wandering mode). What is recommended to improve these sessions? Simply request participants to either prepare ideas before the meeting or write ideas down at the beginning of the meeting. Then, these ideas are written on a whiteboard or chalkboard, shared, discussed, and voted on. However, there's another key aspect to successful group brainstorming, which was written back in the 1940s.

Alex Osborn, a successful ad agency professional, authored a book on his many creative secrets. In his book, *Your Creative Power*, he outlined the essential rules of a successful brainstorming session. According to Osborn, the most important aspect of these rules was ensuring the absence of criticism and negative feedback during the session. If people were worried that the group might ridicule their ideas, the process would fail. Osborn wrote, "Creativity is so delicate a flower that praise tends to make it bloom while discouragement often nips it in the bud. Forget quality; aim now to get a quantity of answers. When you're through, your sheet of paper may be so full of ridiculous nonsense that you'll be disgusted. Never mind. You're loosening up your unfettered imagination—making your mind deliver."

## • Walk Away

**Ready to re-energize?** You've created a good rough draft, and you're ready to edit your work. What's the best way to prepare to review your masterpiece? Take a break. According to studies, we are unable to concentrate for extended periods of time. Taking a break from work activities replenishes your energy, improves self-control and decision-making, and fuels your productivity.

**How long should the break be?** Fifteen minutes is good. The key is to walk away from your desk and avoid launching into another task or reading a social website. Why? Because it's not only your brain that requires a break, so does your body. What will happen when you return? You should feel recharged and ready to edit.

## • Chief and Editor

**Work like an editing pro with A.P.P.L.E.** Yes, one more acronym! Here's a helpful way to remember the key elements when proofing:

- **A.R.T.** – Attention, Relevance, and Takeaway
- **P**ositive approach
- **P**aragraphs with a mix of sentences
- **L**ayout, appealing to the eye
- **E**dited for grammar, spelling, and punctuation

## • Appropriate Attire

**How do you plan to present your message to the reader?** Is this communication best sent in an e-mail, post, paper letter or memorandum? Reference Chapter 2 on selecting the appropriate vehicle for your communication.

## • Is it Really Important?

**Yes!** You've just completed editing an important communication (e-mail, letter, report). What should you do if the document is of great importance? Ask a colleague to review your work. In addition, if you have the time, review your work again the following day before sending. It's remarkable the impact a "fresh set of eyes" has on the final edit of your masterpiece!

## • Feed Your Mind!

**Our brain gets tired too.** It needs energy to focus! Your brain uses more energy than you'd think. Your brain comprises 2 percent of the body's weight, but consumes more than 20 percent of the daily caloric intake of energy. Yes, it consumes more than any other organ in your body!

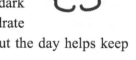

**What foods and beverages are good for your brain?** The brain loves water! Some of its favorite foods are as follows: walnuts, blueberries, olive oil, broccoli, beets, dark chocolate, spinach, and fish. Feed and hydrate your mind! Eating small meals throughout the day helps keep you focused and happy.

# Chapter 9

# Scrubbing Works for Clarity

**T**he beauty of clear writing. As writers, our objective is simple—we want the reader to understand us. However, the act of composing our thoughts, facts, and ideas in a coherent style is often challenging. Let's begin with the number of words we have available for composition. According to *The Global Language Monitor*, the English language passed the million-word threshold on June 10, 2009. The seemingly endless number of words is not the only challenge in composing. It's also the hundreds of grammar and punctuation rules we apply to give structure to our writing. We spend years in school expanding our vocabulary and learning these rules to improve our ability to compose. Don't you find it surprising that you know why to use a particular verb form or understand why a comma "goes there," but you can't remember the rules? Let's be honest, who would ever want to sit for hours in a classroom and learn the forms of the verb *to be* again!

**The business world has even more rules.** *The Gregg Reference Manual* contains more than 600 pages of instruction for composing and formatting business correspondence. This guidebook includes instruction that ranges from the rules of punctuation for titles to abbreviations of business terms. The manual even includes an entire section dedicated to formatting numbers.

And finally, another reason why composition is so challenging is there are many different ways you can explain a concept, define an idea, or get your point across. Hence, you can easily understand why the English language is so complex!

**Did I miss some?** You may find you've forgotten a rule or two on sentence structure or word usage. This chapter reviews the most common "lost" instructions in writing clear and concise correspondence.

## • The Ultimate Control in Writing

**The active and passive voice.** Understanding the power of voice gives you the ultimate control in composition: choosing how to convey your message. Voice indicates whether the subject acts or is acted upon. In the sentences below, compare the difference between the *active voice* and the *passive voice*.

| Active Voice | Passive Voice |
|---|---|
| *Steve* bought a coffee. | The coffee was bought by *Steve*. |
| *Bonnie* called each account. | Each account was called by *Bonnie*. |
| *Mac* made a decision. | A decision was made by *Mac*. |
| The *president* promoted Jake. | Jake was promoted by the president. |

**What's the difference?** The active voice is more conversational, because its conciseness and directness make it a stronger form of expression than the passive voice. The active voice is often easier to read because the focus of the sentence is the *action* of the *subject*. For example:

> The *Heritage Construction Company* refurbished the building.

Here, in the active voice, the *Heritage Construction Company* is both the subject and the doer of the act in the sentence. Now:

> The building was refurbished by the *Heritage Construction Company*.

Here, in the more formal passive voice, the subject is acted upon, which gives *the building* more immediate attention and presents the Heritage Construction Company itself as comparatively unimportant or unknown.

**What are you looking to achieve?** If you seek to state the action of the subject, your choice is simple: the active voice. If the action of the subject is unimportant or unknown, use the passive voice. What's intriguing about the passive voice? You can also use the passive voice if you seek to *avoid* stating the subject's action.

**Which example would you use?** You are the director of graphics for a company that develops packaging for its clients. You must send a message to your boss explaining why a project will not be completed by Friday. Compare the versions: version A is written in the *active voice*, and version B is written in the *passive voice*. Which message would you send?

### Version A - active voice

Unfortunately, the design team is unable to complete the project by Friday. Megan is finalizing the copy, and Scott is revising the final graphics. Megan and Scott require another week to finish the project.

### Version B - passive voice

Unfortunately, the project will not be completed by Friday. The copywriting and graphics have not been finalized. The project requires another week to be completed.

**And your answer is . . . .** In Version A, the subjects and their actions are stated in each sentence. However, in Version B, the passive voice removes the subjects to reveal the same information, but does not make clear to the boss who is responsible for completing which tasks.

### Advantages of Active Voice and Passive Voice

| Active Voice | Passive Voice |
|---|---|
| ✓ Conversational | ✓ Formal |
| ✓ More direct | ✓ Less direct |
| ✓ Stronger form of expression | ✓ Removes responsible subject (optional) |

## • Conversational Writing is Comfortable

**Have you noticed the style throughout this book?** It speaks to you. Rather than a textbook that instructs in a more formal style, this book uses a conversational style. Why is this significant? According to a study on computer-based education, people learn easier from a conversational style than a formal style. Compare Versions A, B, and C. Which version do you prefer?

### Version A – too formal

Dear Brian:

The outcome of the consumer insights research conducted on the current line of bathing products, Lavender Lush, found consumers preferred the liquid soap over the bar soap, 2 to 1. This research will have a significant impact on our proposed production strategy. Therefore, a meeting will be held with the Production Department to ensure this research is included in the development of the production strategy. A meeting invitation will be sent by Ms. Kathy Jones, Director of Production.

Best regards,

Alison

### Version B – conversational

Dear Brian:

We have surprising results from our consumer insights research on Lavender Lush. Customers prefer the liquid soap over the bar soap, 2 to 1. With these results, let's meet to discuss a revised production strategy. Please accept this meeting invitation.

Best regards,

Alison

As version B shows, you can convey the same information with a more lively tone, as well as a statement that is brief. However, be careful not to send fragmented sentences that appear too "texty."

### Version C – too "texty"

Hey Brian, guess what, the study on Lush found people like liquid better. Let's meet. - Alison

# T.H.I.N.K. MORE

## The Brain on Words

**Like waves on a beach. Stop.** Do you know what just occurred? As you read the words, you visualized a wave or a beach and maybe even a stop sign in your mind. Why? Your brain is a highly complex visual machine, which was developed to capture images to support your survival. Therefore, the reason why we find reading so challenging is that our mind sees words as tiny pictures. We view each word independently and verify it before we move to the next.

Though, this visualization is not all that's happening in your mind. As you read and listen to words that describe a particular action, your brain seeks to simulate the experience. Your vision system in your brain recreates what the action would be like; in other words, the brain appears to be taking words and translating them into things we can see, hear, or do. As you can see (no pun intended!), as with writing, the act of reading is complex.

## • The Smooth Sound of Parallel Construction

**Easy reading.** Our minds find text easier to assimilate when we use parallel construction. In other words, the use of the same pattern of words to convey that these words or ideas are of equal importance. For instance, you parallel verb forms *to speak*, *to write*, *to send*, or *speaking, writing, sending*. Why shouldn't you mix "apples and oranges" when it comes to grammatical forms? You'll find the flow of a sentence will sound choppy when you mix these forms. The following examples easily demonstrate the difference between smooth and choppy.

### Example 1

***not parallel*** *(sounds choppy)*
In preparation for the meeting, Betty met with Jack, was calling the caterer, and ordered balloons.
***parallel*** *(smooth sailing)*
In preparation for the meeting, Betty met with Jack, called the caterer, and ordered balloons.

### Example 2

***not parallel*** *(doesn't flow well)*
Our new doll walks, will eat, and can even start crying.
***parallel*** *(a beautiful stream)*
Our new doll walks, eats, and cries.

### Example 3 - Keep lists parallel too!

| *not parallel* | *parallel* |
| --- | --- |
| We guarantee the following: | We guarantee the following: |
| Service that's quick | Quick service |
| Friendly associates | Friendly associates |
| Expected low rates | Low rates |
| A great product list | Excellent products |

## • The Maddening Misplaced Modifier

**Hey, it just sounds complicated.** This error happens when a modifier, word(s) or phrase, is not placed next to the word(s) it modifies. Review the examples below:

### Example 1

*misplaced modifier*
Overwhelmed by the response, the website was receiving hundreds of orders, so Damien called his supervisor. (The website was overwhelmed?)

*correct*

The website was receiving hundreds of orders; overwhelmed by the response, Damien called his supervisor.

**Example 2**

*misplaced modifier*

Nervously, after her speech, she walked off the stage.

*correct*

Nervously, she walked off the stage after her speech.

## • Be Wary of "Day-Old" Clichés

**In a jiffy.** A cliché is a phrase or opinion that expresses a popular thought or idea that is no longer original or interesting. In fact, such phrases can sound downright boring! To ensure that your works possess clarity for your reader, avoid clichés in your letters, memos, and e-mails. Here are some popular clichés to avoid:

- Time will tell
- Read between the lines
- What goes around comes around
- A diamond in the rough
- The writing on the wall
- Bite the bullet

## • The Power of the Idiom

**Word of mouth.** Idioms are common expressions that have a different meaning from the dictionary definitions of their individual words. Idioms are appropriate for business when you have a good working relationship with a colleague, client, or vendor; but avoid using them in formal writing, especially international correspondence. The following is a list of common idioms:

- Win-win situation
- Ahead of the curve
- Back to square one
- See eye-to-eye
- Raise the bar
- No-brainer

Here are a few business idioms for laughing purposes only:

- Putting lipstick on a pig
- Eating our own dog food
- Drinking from a fire hose

## • You're Welcome to Use Contractions!

**I'd be happy to help.** Your writing is easier to understand when you use contractions, which express your meaning quickly. Here are a few examples:

| Full form | Contraction |
|-----------|-------------|
| I would | I'd |
| Let us | Let's |
| You would | You'd |
| You are | You're |
| I am | I'm |
| She is | She's |
| He would | He'd |

## • Transitional Expressions: Writing's Bridge

**Overall.** You can improve the clarity of your written works with transitional expressions. These words help your reader transition from the preceding thought to a newly introduced idea. In the sentences below, transitional expressions appear in italics.

**Example 1**

*As a rule*, we do not allow employees to take a four-week vacation. *However*, due to your extraordinary contributions, we will make an exception.

**Example 2**

*In conclusion*, the owners of the new beverage company will have a stock offering in early December. *Afterward*, they plan to initiate a national ad campaign.

## • OMG or Oh My Goodness?

**BTW.** Texting has opened up a wonderful new use of abbreviations. In the past, the most commonly used abbreviations were business terms, such as "AP" (accounts payable), "dept." (department), or "FYI" (for your information). Today, hundreds of abbreviations are used. For business correspondence, seek to keep the abbreviations business only. You don't want to give the wrong impression where someone would LOL (laugh out loud)!

## • Those Often Confusing Words

**Witch/Which?** Those creators of the English language certainly ensured we would be perplexed at times: a number of words can be very confusing. Though *witch* and *which* are easy to decipher, the following are words that can be challenging when writing.

### Affect/Effect

*Affect* is a verb meaning to "influence change, assume" or a noun meaning "expressing feeling or emotion." *Effect* can be either a noun meaning "result, impressions" or a verb meaning "to bring about."

• The vice president's idea did not *affect* (change) the

timing of the announcement.

- The announcement of the new director will *affect* (feeling) the team's morale.
- Once the director was introduced, he mentioned the *effects* (results) of his new plan.
- We expect our new director to have a positive *effect* (bring about) on the bottom line.

### Among/Between

Use *between* when referring to two persons or things. Use *among* when referring to more than two persons or things.

- The award for the new product idea will be divided *between* Joe and Paula.
- The responsibilities for managing the fund will be divided *among* the seven directors.

### Bad/Badly

Use the adjective *bad* after the verb "feel" or "look." *Badly* is an adverb used to modify verbs, which answers the question of how the action occurred.

- I feel *bad* about the poor service you received.
- She was hurt *badly*.

### Can/May

*May* implies permission. *Can* refers to ability or knowledge.

- *May* I receive a copy of the latest financial report?
- I *can* understand why you were unable to meet me, but why didn't you call me?

### Compliment/Complement

A *compliment* is an expression of praise. A *complement* is something that completes something else.

- Thank you for the *compliment* (praise) on the design of the brochure.

- Your photographs are a *complement* to (completion of) the design of the catalog.

### Couldn't care less/Could care less

When you do not care at all about a particular matter, always use *couldn't care less*. If you *could care less*, it means you care at least a little.

### Ensure/Insure

*Ensure* means to make certain, safe, or secure. To *insure* means to protect against loss (take out an insurance policy on a house, a car, one's life or health, etc.).

- We will *ensure* you're comfortable during your stay at our spa.

- I will *insure* the new house against fire damage or loss.

### Farther/Further

*Farther* refers to actual distance. *Further* refers to figurative distance and means "to a greater degree."

- After driving for two hours, they realized the location was much *farther* than expected.

- During the presentation, they were able to examine the issue *further*.

### Fewer/Less

*Less* refers to a degree or amount and is used with singular nouns. *Fewer* refers to a number and is used with plural nouns.

- Our new coffee maker allows us to use *less* coffee and *fewer* filters.

**Good/Well**

*Good* is an adjective. *Well* is typically an adverb, but may be used as an adjective to refer to the state of someone's health.

- Jason received a *good* report on the marketing campaign initiative. (adjective)

- Shawn did *well* on the management test. (adverb)

- I'm feeling *well*. Thank you for asking. (adjective)

**Maybe/May Be**

*Maybe* is an adverb meaning "perhaps" or "possibly." *May be* is a verb phrase meaning "might be" or "could be."

- If I don't get approval to take July off, *maybe* I'll take August off instead.

- I *may be* out of the office during the month of July.

# Chapter 10

# Rethinking Grammar

**Y**ou **first met in elementary school.** The relationship may have been a struggle in the beginning. Nevertheless, eventually you worked it out and have been together since. Of course, this particular relationship is the one you formed with the rules of grammar and punctuation! What were you thinking? Over the years, you may have found that the features of these many rules may have disappeared from your memory in regard to formal names and definitions. Here's an opportunity for you to rethink the grammar rules in your head and reacquaint yourself with a refresher course that can have a powerful effect on your composition skills. Like a good workout, we'll start slowly with an understanding of the sentence and its parts. With the knowledge of the parts of the sentence, you may find you're able to use more sentence types in your writing and be more confident with punctuation.

129

## • The Sentence

**What is a simple sentence?** It's simple. A simple sentence consists of a *subject* and a *predicate*, which expresses a complete thought. The subject is the noun(s) or pronoun(s) that acts as the topic of a sentence. A predicate is the other part of the sentence, which contains the main verb and tells you what is happening to the subject.

> **A simple sentence can contain a one-word subject and predicate.**
>
> Susie *drove.*
>
> subject *predicate*

> **The subject can consist of more than one word.**
>
> Susie, our operations manager, *drove.*
>
> subject                                   *predicate*

> **The predicate can be more than one word.**
>
> Susie, our manager, *drove to the beach instead of the office.*
>
> subject                           *predicate*

## • Sentence Parts: Clause and Phrase

**What's the difference between a clause and a phrase?** There are two elements of the sentence that are very helpful to know, especially to better understand the rules of punctuation. You know their names, yet you may have forgotten their definitions. Let's get a little closer to the sentence by learning about the *clause* and the *phrase*.

**What's a clause?** Like a simple sentence, a clause also contains a subject and a predicate, yet a clause is part of a full sentence. There are two types of clauses—*independent* and *dependent*.

**The "I'll do it myself" clause.** An independent clause is easy to identify, because it can stand alone as a simple sentence, and it expresses a complete thought. The examples below are sentences that contain two independent clauses (independent clauses are underlined).

<u>We agreed that Las Vegas is a great place for the national sales meeting</u>, and <u>I plan to suggest it to the board</u>.

<u>You've won a trip to Bermuda</u>; in addition, <u>all of your expenses will be paid</u>.

**The "needy" clause.** A dependent clause consists of a subject and a predicate; yet it cannot stand alone as a simple sentence, because it does not express a complete thought (dependent clauses are in italics).

*While Patrick William was speaking*, we were writing.

*When everyone arrives*, you can begin the presentation.

**What's a phrase?** A *phrase* is a group of two or more words that lack either a subject or a predicate or both. A phrase can act as a noun, adjective, or adverb in a sentence. Do you need to know all of these types of phrases? Absolutely not. However, having a general idea of the definition of a phrase is helpful. The phrases in the following sentences appear in italics.

*The idea to open before 6 a.m.* was Dave's. (adjective phrase)

*Opening before 6 a.m.* is how we attract our best customers. (noun phrase)

We wanted to meet *after dinner*. (adverbial phrase)

*From Maine to Florida*, we deliver our goods daily. (prepositional phrase)

*To exit quickly*, you press the button labeled, "Finished." (infinitive phrase)

The marketing head *considering your proposal* is calling. (participle phrase)

## • Types of Sentences

**You've got options.** Again, there are a number of sentence types you can choose from: below is an overview of commonly used sentences. The good news is you're already familiar with the first one listed!

A **simple sentence** consists of a subject and a predicate:

<u>The Gingham and Jones Group</u> *has accepted our offer.*

<u>subject</u>                                        *predicate*

A **compound sentence** contains two or more independent clauses, which are underlined in the following examples:

<u>She wrote it</u>; therefore, <u>I'll mail it</u>.

<u>The members of the committee are meeting at 2 p.m. to review recommendations</u>, and <u>they will announce their decision soon.</u>

A **complex sentence** consists of an independent clause (underlined) and one or more dependent clauses (in italics):

*Once we presented our plan*, <u>we knew it would be approved.</u>

<u>Audrey will have to wait in the office</u>, *until he arrives.*

A **compound-complex sentence** consists of one or more dependent clauses (*italics*) and two independent clauses (underlined):

*As Colin enjoyed his coffee*, <u>he read the latest reports from the manufacturing division</u>, and <u>he was pleased to learn the division will meet all retailer delivery dates for the month.</u>

## • Joining Clauses in Sentences

**Looking for ways to join your clauses?** There are three options available in joining your clauses, which are (1) *conjunctions*, (2) *transitional expressions*, and (3) *punctuation*. The following is an overview of each.

**(1) What's your function, Mr. Conjunction?** *Conjunctions* can be used to join words, phrases, and clauses, which are *and, but, yet, or,* and *nor.* Conjunctions appear in *italics* in the following examples:

The train broke down, *and* he was late for work.

Do you prefer to meet in the conference room, *or* do you want to meet at the coffee shop?

**(2) Transitional expressions bridge your clauses.** Another great way to join clauses is with a *transitional expression.* Again, these words and phrases allow you to help the reader transition from one thought to the next. Below are six common types of transitional expressions to join clauses.

**Addition:** *additionally, furthermore, in addition, moreover*

The engine is not operating efficiently; *moreover*, we don't have time to adjust it.

**Explaining:** *although, at the same time, but, however, nevertheless, regardless*

I'm unable to meet you this morning; *however*, I can meet you for lunch.

**Providing an example:** *for example, specifically*

We will purchase a pallet of spring water; *specifically*, I'd like the Vermont brand.

**Showing cause and effect:** *as a result, because, therefore*

The copier is broken; *as a result*, I'm going to the office store to print this report.

**Summarizing:** *briefly, in any case, in short, in summary*

Logan said we'll meet the production timeline; *in short*, Lenny will be pleased.

**Timing:** *afterward, as soon as, in the meantime, since, until*

Please use the black pens the supplier shipped; *in the meantime*, I'll contact them to ship you a box of blue pens.

### (3) Punctuation is a great way to shorten a sentence.

The semicolon and colon can be used in place of conjunctions and transitional expressions. You'll learn more about these marks at the end of the chapter.

**The semicolon.** Use a semicolon, rather than a comma and a conjunction, to join two independent clauses. The clauses must be closely related.

**Smart Punctuation!**

I'm planning to finish the report by noon; Lindsey is going to distribute it.

OR: I'm planning to finish the report by noon, *and* Lindsey is going to distribute it.

During the conference, Claudia spoke on the importance of volunteering; she urged us to donate our time to charity.

OR: During the conference, Claudia spoke on the importance of volunteering, *and* she urged us to donate our time to charity.

**The colon.** Substitute a conjunction or transitional expression with a colon when the second independent clause explains the first independent clause.

I plan to purchase new cars for our sales representatives: the cost of each car is $40K.

OR: I plan to purchase new cars for our sales representatives, *and* the cost of each car is $40K.

Her speech was very moving: I wept during the opening.

OR: Her speech was very moving; *as a result*, I wept during the opening.

# T.H.I.N.K. MORE

## Why Don't We Remember All the Rules?

**We often lose 90 percent!** So, why don't we remember all of the rules of grammar? The answer is how we memorize declarative information, such as grammar rules. According to John Medina, developmental molecular biologist and author, we lose 90 percent of what we learn in a classroom within 30 days. We do the majority of this forgetting within the first few hours after class. However, if you repeat lessons learned within the first few minutes, repeat them again within the first few hours, and then once more within the first 30 days, the chances of you memorizing them are improved.

**Looking for help to memorize something new?** Consider the "3, 3, 30 Plan." Write the information down within the first 3 minutes, write it down again within the first 3 hours, and write it down again within the first 30 days.

## • Adding Variety to Your Works

**Do you like variety?** What if M&M's were all brown? It's the variety of colors that makes those yummy candies more enjoyable. What if the only sentence available to compose was one that consisted of just a subject and predicate? Compare the paragraphs below, and consider which one you find easier to read.

### Simple sentences only

Jack, please forward your copy of the Gifford House Project plans to Kerry by Thursday. She would like to contact Mr. and Mrs. Gifford on Monday. There are concerns about the layout of the kitchen. Kerry would like to rework the plans. She would also like to meet with them next week. She wants to review a new layout for the dining area. This layout is a critical issue. It may alter our timeline.

### A variety of sentences

Jack, please forward your copy of the Gifford Project plans to Kerry by Thursday, because she would like to contact Mr. and Mrs. Gifford on Monday. There are concerns about the layout of the kitchen: Kerry would like to rework the plans. She would also like to meet with them next week to review a new layout for the dining area; overall, this layout is a critical issue that may alter our timeline.

**Looking to spice up your works?** On the following page, you'll find a great reference guide for the top ten sentence types. Enjoy!

# The Top Ten Sentences

**1. Simple Sentence**
Sandy drove to work.

**2. Compound sentence joined with a conjunction.**
Sandy drove to work, and she picked up Dave at his home.

**3. Compound sentence joined with a transitional expression.**
Sandy stopped at the coffee shop; in addition, she bought Dave a coffee.

**4. Dependent clause and an independent clause.**
Unless Sandy asks, Dave won't give her money for driving costs or coffee.

**5. Independent clause and a dependent clause.**
Sandy wishes Dave would pay for some of the expenses before it's too late.

**6. Dependent clause, independent clause, transitional expression, and an independent clause.**
When they arrived at the office, Sandy asked Dave for gas money; however, Dave told her he never carries cash.

**7. Words in a series.**
Sandy told Dave that he owed her for purchasing gas, buying coffee, and paying for tolls.

**8. Introductory modifier with an independent clause.**
Quickly, Dave told Sandy he would call her about it later.

**9. One word sentence.**
Call. (*you* is implied)

**10. Introductory prepositional phrase, independent clause, transitional expression, and another independent clause.**
At 7 a.m. the next day, Dave stood outside his home; nevertheless, Sandy waved as she drove by his home.

# Punctuation

**For most of us, punctuation can be painful.** Let's be honest—there are just too many rules! To help refresh your memory, here's a guide to the basics of punctuation: the *comma*, *semicolon*, and *colon*. You may have to review these rules more than three times, but once you have the rules memorized, you'll be an expert! Let's begin with the punctuation mark that's often more confusing than rocket science—the comma.

## • The Comma

**Controlling the comma.** With the amount of messaging that does not include commas, you'd think the comma would have been filed away in an old cabinet. Yet, we must keep this important mark alive. Here are a few examples of why this punctuation mark continues to be strong.

### A world without commas

Woman without her man is nothing.
Please purchase name cards green pens and notebooks.
It's time to eat Brooks.

### A world with commas

Woman: without her, man is nothing.
Please purchase name cards, green pens, and notebooks.
It's time to eat, Brooks.

**The two jobs of the comma.** A comma has two basic jobs: (1) *to set off* nonessential expressions that interrupt the flow of thought, and (2) *to separate* elements within a sentence to clarify their relationship with one another. The following are the rules to separate elements within a sentence.

## • Commas to Separate

**Numbers.** A comma is used to separate digits greater than 999:

1,350 jumbo paper clips    $95,000 in unmarked bills

**Adjectives.** A comma is used to separate two consecutive adjectives that modify a noun. To know whether or not adjectives need to be separated, substitute the word *and* for the comma:

The boss is an intelligent, wonderful person.

OR: The boss is an intelligent *and* wonderful person.

Pork and beans are a delightful, tasty meal.

OR: Pork and beans are a delightful *and* tasty meal.

Keep it together! Do not separate adjectives that describe age, size, number, color, or location:

We just ordered 27 blue notebooks and 74 yellow pencils for the entire office.

**Omission of *that*.** A comma can be used to replace the word *that* in a sentence:

Keep in mind, the Internet never shuts down.

OR: Keep in mind *that* the Internet never shuts down.

Please note, the new vacation policy begins January 1.

OR: Please note *that* the new vacation policy begins January 1.

**Words in a series.** Commas are used to separate words, phrases, and clauses forming a series:

To deliver the speech, we must choose amongst the president, vice president, or CEO.

Carla, please order 12 turkey subs, 10 salads, and 2 cakes.

**Independent clauses.** Commas are used to separate two independent clauses when they are joined by a coordinating conjunction (*and, but, yet, or, nor*):

> We are thrilled about receiving 1,026 orders for our new penguin pencil poppers, *but* we do not believe the orders can be filled in time for the holidays.

**Introductory elements.** A comma is used to separate introductory word(s), phrases, or dependent clauses:

> *Look*, Ken knows he will be promoted soon.

> *Once Judy opens our new store in Dallas*, I'll send her a welcome basket.

## • Commas to Set Off

**You don't need it, so set it off.** You just reviewed the complex uses of the comma. Now, you'll review the comma that simply sets off nonessential elements in a sentence. What's a nonessential element? These are words or phrases that are not essential to the meaning of the sentence; therefore, commas are used to set them off.

**Year and geographical location or address.** Commas are used to set off the year and town/city location in a sentence:

> On April 22, *2065*, we will be open for business.

> The new store is located at 22 Main Street, *Wellesley*, Massachusetts.

**Words of direct address and interjections.** Apply the comma to set off words of direct address or interjections that are considered nonessential:

> *Eric*, will you call me when you have a moment?

> *Wow*, the coffee tastes awesome!

**Descriptive information.** Use commas to set off nonessential descriptive information known as an appositive, which is a noun or noun substitute that describes the noun preceding it (in business, the most popular appositive is a person's title):

Jimmy, *the CEO*, wet his pants again.

The new copier, *located on the second floor*, is out of paper again. Please ask Robert to refill it immediately.

**Transitional expressions.** Overall, these powerful words help bridge ideas in your writing. They are also nonessential elements:

Mary was relieved, *nonetheless*, to discover Tom won the sales award. She won't have to hear him complain anymore.

**Afterthoughts and comments.** These additional thoughts and comments are also set off with commas:

You did receive the paperwork on time, *didn't you*?

Would you please forward the file to Tim, *thank you*.

**Elements that interrupt.** Elements that interrupt are sometimes the cause of breaks in the flow of sentences. These words do not have a formal name, yet they are set off with commas:

Mr. Sterling, *not Mr. Jones*, will host the golf tournament at Bushwood this summer.

Fashion design today, *unlike the '70s*, is a free-for-all.

## • The Semicolon
**Take hold of the power of this wonderful mark.** Now that you have a good grasp of the comma, you may find the semicolon is

easy to apply. Use a semicolon for the following:

**Independent clauses.** If a greater break is necessary between two independent clauses, use a semicolon before the coordinating conjunction:

> The product briefs were e-mailed to our London office; but the samples were sent via overnight mail to the Boston office.

> The crop report for this year is expected to be good; and we plan to profit.

Use a semicolon when independent clauses are not joined with a coordinating conjunction:

> The new toy samples will arrive before noon today; the equipment samples will arrive on Friday.

**Transitional expressions.** A semicolon is used before and a comma after when two independent clauses are linked with a transitional expression. (The transitional expressions *hence, then, thus, so,* and *yet* do not require a comma to follow unless a stronger pause is needed.)

> All department heads are requested to work 40 hours a week; *that is,* they should work eight hours a day.

> Justin won the lottery; *moreover,* I don't believe he'll be back to work.

**Series.** A semicolon is necessary to separate items in a series when words within each item are already separated with commas. This placement alleviates using too many commas in the sentence.

> The names of our executive team are Tim Whit, President; Nat Whit, CEO; and Al Whit, CFO.

## • **The Colon**

**The greatest pause.** The comma and semicolon ask you to pause; the colon demands you to pause and stop! Like the semicolon, the colon has several rules.

**Series.** Use a colon when a statement or series is introduced by *as follows*, the *following*, or when the latter is implied.

The restaurants in our area feature *the following* cuisines: Italian, French, and Japanese.

The car is equipped with these features:

- Anti-lock brakes
- Airbags
- Leather seats

**Transitional expressions.** A colon precedes and a comma follows the transitional expressions *for example*, *that is*, and *namely* when they introduce a series of words, phrases, or clauses:

During the promotion, the marketing team is planning to give away a great number of items: *for example*, hats, tee shirts, beach towels, and soccer balls.

**Explanatory clause.** Use a colon to separate the first clause and the explanatory clause when they are <u>not</u> joined with a coordinating conjunction or a transitional expression:

The plan is to move the corporate offices: a location in Hawaii is likely.

You'll receive copies of the incident reports: all of these reports are dated 10/22.

# Overview
## The Comma, Semicolon, and Colon
## & Cats and Dogs

 **Looking for an overview?** What are the differences between punctuating independent clauses, a series, or transitional expressions with the comma, semicolon, or colon? Compare the sentences below for each mark with a little help from our four legged friends.

## • Independent Clauses

Use a **comma** to separate two independent clauses when joined with a coordinating conjunction.

> Our dog Bruno is running across the lawn, *and* Maisey the cat is chasing him.

Use a **semicolon** to separate two independent clauses when they are not linked with a coordinating conjunction.

> Bruno is running across the lawn; Maisey is chasing him.

Use a **colon** to separate an independent clause from an explanatory clause.

> Bruno is running across the lawn: he is afraid of cats, especially Maisey.

## • Series of Words

Use a **comma** to separate words, phrases, or clauses in a series.

> The names of their dogs are Gigi, Cooper, Theo, and Sheba.

Use a **semicolon** when there are too many commas to separate in a series.

The names and birth dates of the dogs are Gigi, January 1; Cooper, July 4; Theo, December 25; and Sheba, August 22.

Place a **colon** before such expressions as *for example, namely*, and *that is* when they introduce words, phrases, or a series of clauses anticipated earlier in the sentence.

The owners of the dogs ensure their pets are pampered: *for example*, the dogs are groomed, taken for walks, and fed twice daily.

## • Transitional Expressions

**Commas** are used to set off a transitional expression when it interrupts the flow of the sentence.

Bruno, *however*, jumped up on the couch onto his owner's lap to escape Maisey.

A **semicolon** and **comma** are used to set off a transitional expression when it joins two independent clauses.

Bruno cuddled up with his owner on the couch; *although*, Maisey sat on the floor.

Use a **colon** even if the anticipatory expression is only implied and not stated.

The owners of Maisey provided her with smart accessories: a diamond collar, a luxurious scratching post, and a tracking device.

# NOTES

Thank you to all of the researchers, writers, scientists, doctors, journalists, and artists for their supporting ideas brought forth in this book.

## Quotes

ix  Einstein, Albert (Werthmeimer, 1959, 213: Pais, 1982).

ix  Gates, Bill (2000, October 18). Keynote address at the Creating Digital Dividends Conference in Seattle, WA.

ix  Jobs, Steve (1994, June 16). *Rolling Stone* interview.

ix  Watson, Jr., Thomas J. (1957). IBM Corporate Archives.

## Introduction

xii  Maslow, Abraham (1954). *Motivations and Personality* New York, NY: Harper.

xii  Medina, John (2009, March 31*). Brain Rules: 12 Principles for Surviving and Thriving at Work, Home, and School*, Second Edition. Edmonds, Washington: Pear Press.

xiii  Whitebourne Krauss, Ph.D., Susan (2012, June 30). The Ultimate Guide to Body Language. *Psychology Today* Retrieved from http://psychologytoday.com

xv  Kaku, Michio (2012, February 21). *Physics of the Future: How Science will Shape Human Destiny and Our Daily Lives by the Year 2100*. London: Allen Lane.

## Chapter One

1    IBM Archives. Retrieved from https: //www 03.ibcom ibm/history/exhibits/attic2/attic2_207.html

4    Prince (1982). "1999." *1999*: Warner Brothers Records.

5    iPhone is a registered trademark of Apple, Inc.

6    Bradt, Steve (2010, November 11). Wandering Mind Not a Happy Mind. *Harvard Gazette*. Retrieved from http://news.harvard.edu/gazette

6    Ostrach, Teresia R. (1997). Typing Speed: How Fast is Average? Five Star Staffing, Inc., Orlando, FL.

8    Mehrabian, Albert, Ph.D. (1972, July). *Silent Messages*. Belmont, CA: Wadsworth Publishing Company.

10  Mark, Gloria J.; Voida, Stephen; and Cardello, Armand V. (2012, May). *A Pace Not Dictated By Electrons: An Empirical Study of Work Without E-mail*. Department of Informatics at the University of California, Irvine, CA, and U.S. Army Natick Soldier R, D & E Center, Natick, MA.

11  Brown, Chris; Killick, Andrew; Renaud, Karen (2013 September). To Reduce E-mail, Start at the Top. *Harvard Business Review*. Retrieved from https://hbr.org/2013/09/to-reduce-e-mail-start-at-the-top

12  Rolling Stones (1978). *Some Girls*: Umvd Labels.

12  Bruce Springsteen & The E-Street Band (2001). *Bruce Springsteen & The E-Street Band Live In NYC*: Sony.

14  FindLaw (2015). Email Privacy Concerns. Retrieved from http://consumer.findlaw.com/online-scams/email-privacy-concerns

15  Martin, Andrew (2007, July 12). Whole Foods Executive Used Alias. *The New York Times*. Retrieved from http://nytimes.com

17  Radicati, PhD., Sara (2014). *Email Statistics Report,*

2014-2018. The Radicati Group, Inc. Palo Alto, CA.

17 Mark, Gloria J.; Gudith, Daniela; and Klocke, Ulrich (April 2008). *The Cost of Interrupted Work: More Speed and Stress.* Department of Informatics at the University of California, Irvine, CA, and Institute of Psychology-Humboldt University, Berlin, Germany.

17 Levitin, Daniel J. (2014, August 19). *The Organized Mind: Thinking Straight in the Age of Information Overload.* New York, NY: The Penguin Group.

18 Thompson, Hugh and Sullivan, Bob (2013, May 3). Brain, Interrupted Buzz! Ding! Ding! Rrring! *The New York Times.* Retrieved from http://www.nytimes.com

19 Pattison, Kermit (2008, July 28). Worker, Interrupted: The Cost of Task Switching. *Fast Company.* Retrieved from https://www.fastcompany.com/944128/worker-interrupted-cost-task-switching.

20 Begley, Sharon (2011, March 7). I Can't Think! *Newsweek*, 28-33.

21 Stothard, Cary (2015, August). The Attentional Cost of Receiving a Cell Notification, *Journal of Experimental Psychology*: Human Perception and Performance.

21 Dokoupil, Tony (2012, July 16). Tweets, Texts, Email, Posts: Is the On Slaught Making Us Crazy? *Newsweek, 24-30.*

21 Berridge, Kent C. and Robinson, Terry E. (1998, June 23). What is the Role of Dopamine in Reward: Hedonic Impact, Reward Learning, or Incentive Salience? *Brain Research Reviews*, 309-369.

21 Weinschenk, Ph.D., Susan (2012, September 11). Why We're All Addicted to Texts, Twitter, and Google. *Psychology Today.* Retrieved from http://psychologytoday.com

24 Bounds, Gwendolyn (2010, October 5). How Handwriting Trains the Brain. *The Wall Street Journal.* Retrieved

from http://wsj.com

24  Mueller, P.A. and Oppenheimer, D.M. (2014, January 16). *The Pen is Mightier than the Keyboard: Advantages of Longhand Over Laptop Note Taking*. Los Angeles and New Jersey: Princeton University and the University of California.

24  Jones, Bruce (2014, June 18). Creativity Challenged? Add a Right-Brain Warm Up To Your Daily "To-Do" List. Retrieved from http://Disneyinstitute.com

25  Brown, Sunni (2014, January 9). *The Doodle Revolution: Unlock the Power to Think Differently*, New York, New York: Portfolion Hardcover.

25  CNN (2013, October 29). Doodling in a Meeting? Maybe You're Just Drawing Inspiration. Interview with Sunni Brown.

27  Samp (United Sample) (2011, May 18). Collaboration & Social Tools Drain Business Productivity, Costing Millions in Work Interruptions. Milpitas, CA: harmon.ie. Retrieved from http://harmon.ie/company/press release

28  Williams, Pharrell (2014, March 3). "Happy." *Girl*: Sony.

## Chapter 2

29  Seppälä, Ph.D., Emma (2014, September 29). What Email Does to Your Brain. *Psychology Today*. Retrieved from  http://psychologytoday.com

30  *The Shape of E-mail Research Report* (2012, June). Retrieved from Mimecast.com.

30  Spira, John B. (2005, September). *The Cost of Not Paying Attention*: How Interruptions Impact Knowledge Worker Productivity. basex. New York, NY. Retrieved from http://static1.1.sqspcdn.com/static/f/906912/21655082/1358311185020/Basex-+Cost+Of+Not+Paying+Attention+Report.pdf?to-

ken=vTzWHA0wzo8%2FpMf2PKADM8C2wmk%3D

30  Mark, Gloria J.; Gonzalez, Victor M.; and Harris, Justin (2005, April). *No Task Left Behind? Examining the Nature of Fragmented Work.* Donald Bren School of Information and Computer Sciences at the University of California, Irvine, CA. Retrieved at https://www.ics.uci.edu/~gmark/CHI2005.pdf

31  U.S. Bureau of Labor Statistics (2016). Household Data, Annual Averages. Median weekly earnings of management, business, professional, and related occupations. The average hourly earnings are $27.42. Retrieved from http://www.bls.gov/news.release/pdf/empsit.pdf

35  Weinschenk, Ph.D., Susan (2012, September 11). Why We're All Addicted to Texts, Twitter, and Google. *Psychology Today.* Retrieved from Retrieved from http://psychologytoday.com

37  The Creative Group (2009, July 8). *DOH! Survey Reveals Worst E-mail Mistakes Made on the Job.* Menlo Park, CA. Retrieved from http://creativegroup.mediaroom.com

38  Porges, Seth (2016, November 16). Hear Only What You Want. *Entrepreneur.*

**Chapter 3**

42  Levitin, Daniel J. (2014, August 19). *The Organized Mind: Thinking Straight in the Age of Information Overload.* New York, NY: The Penguin Group.

46  *Titanic* (1997, December 19). Paramount Pictures.

46  *Toy Story* (1995, November 22). Walt Disney Pictures and Pixar.

48  Dickerson, Kelly (2014, July 1). Stopped in Your Tracks. *Psychology Today.* Retrieved from http://psychologytoday.com

50  Ramos, Harold (1980) *Caddyshack.* Orion Pictures.

Author's note: one of the best movies ever made.

## Chapter 4

62 Wilkins, R.W.; Hodges, D.A.; Laurienti, P.J.; Steen, M.; Burdette, J.H. (2014, October). Network Science and the Effects of Music Preference on Functional Brain Connectivity from Beethoven to Eminem. *Scientific Reports* 4, Article number: 6130.

62 Bloom, Paul (2016, March 23). The Reasons Our Minds Wander. *The Atlantic*. Retrieved from http://www.theatlantic.com/science/archive/2016/03/imagination-as-proxy/474918/

63 David, P.H.D., Susan (2016, November 1). *BottomLine Personal*. Volume 37, Number 21.

63 Carnegie, Dale (1998, October 1). *How to Win Friends and Influence People*. New York, NY: Gallery Books, reprint.

66 DiSalvo, David (2012, November 9). Study: Receiving a Compliment has Same Positive Effect as Receiving Cash. *Forbes*. Retrieved from http://Forbes.com

67 Otani, Akane (2014, October 7). The Five Most Hated Types of Work E-mails. *Bloomberg Businessweek*. Retrieved from http://businessweek.com/articles/2014

69 Miller, George A. (1956). The Magical Number Seven, Plus or Minus Two: Some Limits on our Capacity for Processing Information. Harvard University. *Psychological Review*, 63, 81-97. Retrieved from http://psychclassics.yorku.ca/Miller

70 Newburg, Andrew M.D. and Waldman, Mark Robert (2012, 15 May). *Words Can Change Your Brain: 12 Conversation Strategies to Build Trust, Resolve Conflict, and Increase Intimacy.*: New York, NY: Hudson Street Press.

## Chapter 5

75 Begley, Sharon (2011, March 7). I Can't Think! *Newsweek*, 28-33.

76 Budget Travel (2007, August 25). Spirit CEO: We Owe Him Nothing. Retrieved from Budget.com

77 Markman, Art Ph. D. (2014, June 3). Why Hearing Good News or Bad News First Really Matters. *Psychology Today*. Retrieved from http://psychologytoday.com

80 Newburg, Andrew M.D. and Waldman, Mark Robert (2012, 15 May). *Words Can Change Your Brain: 12 Conversation Strategies to Build Trust, Resolve Conflict, and Increase Intimacy.*: New York, NY: Hudson Street Press.

83 Mankins, Michael C. (2016, February 25). Is Technology Really Helping Us Get More Done? *Harvard Business Review. Retrieved from hbr.com*

## Chapter 6

85 A Short History of the Birth and Growth of the American Office (1998). Smithsonian Education. Retrieved from http://www.smithsonianeducation.org/scitech/carbons/text/birth.html

96 Carlson, Kurt A. and Shu, Suzanne B. (2013, June 10). *When Three Charms but Four Alarms: Identifying the Optimal Number of Claims in Persuasion Settings.* Georgetown University McDonough School of Business and UCLA Anderson School of Management.

96 Whittaker, Steve (2012, May 7-12). *Am I Wasting My Time Organizing Email?* A Study of email Refinding. Retrieved from www.people.ucsc.edu/~swhittak/papers/chi2011_refinding_email camera_ready.pdf.

97 Oxford Economics (2014, February). *An Assessment of Paid Time Off in the U.S. Implications for employ-*

*ees, companies, and the economy.* Oxford Economics. Retrieved from http://www.projecttimeoff.com/sites/ projecttimeoff.com/files/Oxford_UnusedTimeOff_Full-Report.pdf

98 Sabin, William A. (2010, March 1). *The Gregg Reference Manual, Tenth Edition.* New York, NY: McGraw-Hill/ Irwin.

99 *The Gregg Reference Manual, Tenth Edition* (as above.)

100 *The Gregg Reference Manual, Tenth Edition* (as above.)

### Chapter 7

103 Dobrin, Arthur (2014, March 17). PowerPoint Makes You Stupid. *Psychology Today.* Retrieved from http:// psychologytoday.com

### Chapter 8

108 Drummond, Katie (2012, August). The Best Essential Oil for Stress? *Prevention.* Retrieved from Prevention.com.

108 Lee, Kevan (2014, March 14). *The Best Times to Write and Get Ideas, According to Science.* Retrieved from http://blog.bufferapp.com

108 Shannon, B.J., Dosenback; R.A., Su; Y.; Vlassenko, A.G.; Larson-Prior, L.J.; Nolan, T. S.; Snyder, A.Z.; Raichle, M.E.(2013, March 1). *Journal of Neurophysiology,* Volume 109 No. 5, 1444-1456 DOI: 10.1152/jn.00651.201 Retrieved from http://jn.physiology.org

111 Weinschendk, Ph.D., Susan (2013, January 10). Our Minds Wander at Least 30 Percent of the Time. *Psychology Today.* Retrieved from http://psychologytoday.com

112 Greenfield, Rebecca (2014, July 29). Brainstorming Doesn't Work: Try This Technique Instead. *Fast Company.* Retrieved from http://www.fastcompany.com

112 Osborn, Alex (1948). *Your Creative Power*, Scribner.

112 Lehrer, Jonah (2012, January 30). Groupthink The Brainstorming Myth. *The New Yorker.* Retrieved from http://www.newyorker.com/magazine

113 Friedman, Ph.D. Ron (2014, November 10). Want to Get More Done? Start Taking Breaks. *Psychology Today.* Retrieved from http://psychologytoday.com.

**Chapter 9**

116 Sabin, William A. (2010, March 1). *The Gregg Reference Manual, Tenth Edition.* New York, NY: McGraw-Hill/Irwin.

118 Mayer, Richard E.; Fennell, Sherry; Farmer, Lindsay; Campbell, Julie (2004). University of California, Santa Barbara. *A Personalization Effect in Multimedia Learning: Students Learn Better When Words Are in Conversational Style Rather Than Formal Style.* Retrieved from http://tecfa.unige.ch/tecfa/teaching/methodo/Mayer2004.pdf

120 Hamilton, John (2013, May 2). *Imagine A Flying Pig: How Words Take Shape in the Brain.* Retrieved from NPR.com.

124 Blake, Gary and Bly, Robert W. (1992, August 8). *The Elements of Business Writing.* New York, NY: Collier Books, Macmillan Publishing Company.

**Chapter 10**

135 Medina, John (2009, March 31). *Brain Rules: 12 Principles for Surviving and Thriving at Work, Home, and School,* Second Edition. Edmonds, Washington: Pear Press.

138 Sabin, William A. (2010, March 1). *The Gregg Reference Manual, Tenth Edition.* New York, NY: McGraw-Hill/Irwin.

# INDEX

157

Jan Dyer O'Neil began her career in marketing communications on the launch team at a Fortune 500 company. Over the past twenty years, she has been responsible for communicating to hundreds of employees, thousands of retailers, and millions of consumers. Her years of experience in business communication and passion for writing were the catalysts in creating T.H.I.N.K. Jan resides in the Boston area and is the parent of three wonderful sons.

9 781630 475857